Judi Sunderland • Leann Cooke

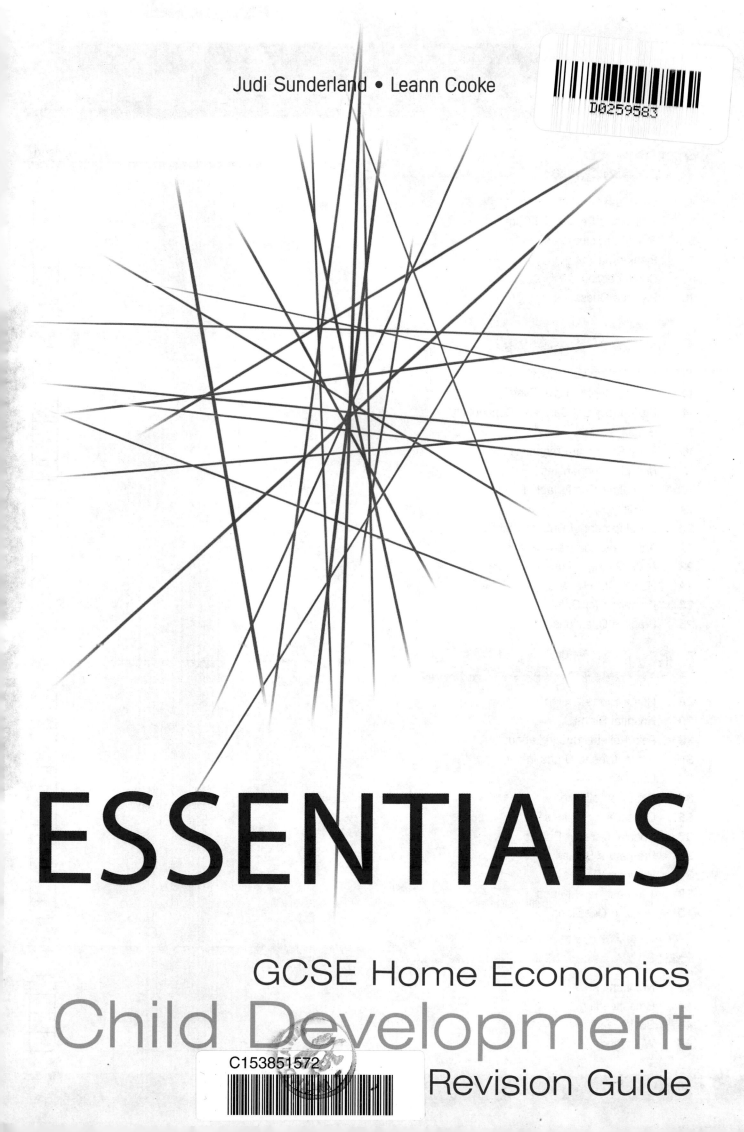

ESSENTIALS

GCSE Home Economics

Child Development

Revision Guide

Contents

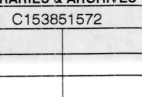

Revised

Contents

What is a Family?

What a Family Provides

A **family** is the **basic unit of society**. It's a group of people living together, who are married, or co-habit (live together), or who are related by birth (blood) or adoption.

A family provides...
- a **secure and stable environment**, with **good role models** and **appropriate routines**
- **encouragement and praise**, which develops self-esteem and confidence
- **love**, **affection** and **comfort**

- **communication skills**
- **food**, **clothing** and a suitable housing environment
- **physical** and **health care**
- **culture**
- **socialisation skills**. Babies' basic needs are met by parents who teach them what is expected of them as they grow. This is **primary socialisation**. Later, they're influenced by the society they live in. This is known as **secondary socialisation**.

Types of Family

There are a number of different types of family.

In a **nuclear family**, parents and children live together in the home. Contact with other family members is limited, and practical help from them isn't easily available.

In an **extended family**, parents and children live with, or near, relatives like grandparents, aunts, uncles and cousins. There is practical help with child care and emotional support.

A **step family** (reconstituted / modified / blended) is formed when one or both people in a couple, with children from a previous relationship, re-marry or co-habit. New relationships can be difficult to establish.

A **single-parent family** (lone, one parent) mostly, but not always, comprises a mother and her children. This type of family can be the result of...
- divorce (separation)
- the death of a parent
- adoption by a single parent
- an absent parent (e.g. who works abroad, is in hospital, or prison, or in refuge)
- a surrogacy arrangement
- a single woman giving birth through choice
- a single woman giving birth after a sexual attack.

In a single-parent family, one parent has responsibility for daily care and decision making. This arrangement may provide a less stressful environment for the children, but can increase pressure on the parent.

In a **shared care family**, children live in two households, and spend time with both parents. Joint decisions are made about them. Children maintain relationships with both parents.

In an **adoptive family**, adoptive parents have to pass rigorous tests by social services. Adoptive parents come from a wide range of backgrounds, such as...
- nuclear families
- single-parent families
- same-sex couples.

Adoptive parents provide a permanent home for babies and older children. A court gives them the same legal rights and responsibilities as birth parents. Reasons for adopting are numerous and include...
- infertility
- adoption after remarriage
- adoption of a family member
- adoption of a disadvantaged child from the UK or abroad
- adoption by couples who carry genetic defects.

Foster and Residential Care

Looked-After Children

Looked-after children are **looked after** by (or are in the care of) the local authority, through social services. This could be the result of a care order or in agreement with the children's parents. Looked-after children have a named social worker.

There are a number of reasons why these children may not be able to live with their birth families, e.g.:
- death or illness of their parents
- sexual or physical abuse or neglect
- if a child has a disability or complex needs
- if parents need respite care.

Looked-after children are placed with **foster families**, or in a **residential care home**. Placements may be short-term, long-term, temporary or permanent.

Foster Families

Foster families provide long or short-term care. Carers are checked by social services, and like adoptive parents they come from many backgrounds. They may be members of the child's birth family.

After training, foster parents are paid by the local authority when children are placed with them.

Foster children have social workers who liaise with the foster family and provide support and advice.

When appropriate, foster children are encouraged to keep in touch with their birth family, with the aim of reuniting them.

Residential Care Homes

Residential care homes provide short-term care for children. They're situated in the local community and small groups of children are looked after by carers in a family type structure. Children with severe disabilities and behavioural problems may require long-term care.

Quick Test

1. In what type of family do parents and children live together?
2. Name two types of socialisation.
3. Who looks after children in a residential care home?
4. Foster carers are paid to look after children. **True** or **false**?

KEY WORDS
Make sure you understand these words before moving on!
- Primary socialisation
- Secondary socialisation
- Nuclear family
- Extended family
- Step family
- Single-parent family
- Shared care family
- Adoptive family
- Looked-after children
- Foster families

Family Structures and Roles

Why are Family Structures Changing?

Family structures are **changing** because...
- unmarried mothers are socially acceptable
- co-habitation is socially acceptable
- divorce laws are simpler

- improved and easily available contraception lets people choose when and how many children they will have
- more benefits and support are available to lone parents.

Family Roles

Roles in a family are complicated, especially after divorce, remarriage and co-habitation. Working mothers have an effect on family roles.

Whether your **sexual role** is decided by **nature** (your genes) or **nurture** (the environment you are brought up in) is debatable. Both are influential.

Stereotyping results from what children see in society and in their homes.

The table shows **traditional expectations**.

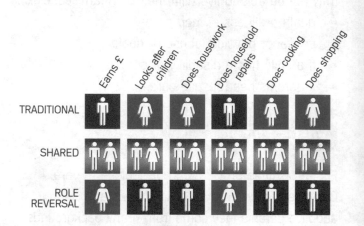

	GIRLS				
GIRLS	To cry if hurt	To be clean, neat and tidy	To be gentle, well-behaved and quiet	To play with dolls and teddies	To dress in pink, frilly clothes
BOYS	To be brave if hurt	To get dirty and grubby	To be physically active, noisy and boisterous	To play with lego and cars	To dress in blue, 'boys' clothes

Culture

Culture has an effect on roles within the family. Culture is behaviour that is learned not only from the family, but also society.

Religion can determine rules of behaviour, provides for worship and celebrations, and can influence your style of dress and diet.

In a multicultural society, like Britain, there are many different **ethnic groups**, each with their own special culture.

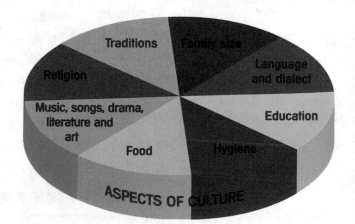

Questions to Consider

Before you decide to have a baby, there are a number of questions to consider.

For example, are you…
- fit and healthy?
- too young or too old?
- mature enough to accept responsibility?
- willing to change your lifestyle?

And do you…
- have a stable relationship with your partner?
- have realistic expectations of children?
- have support from family and friends?
- have sufficient money to buy equipment?
- have suitable housing?
- want any more children?

Bad Reasons for Having a Baby

Bad reasons for having a baby include wanting to…
- have someone to love or look after
- have someone who will love you
- improve a poor or difficult relationship
- prove you are 'grown up' and mature.

Other bad reasons are…
- peer pressure
- family pressure, e.g. from parents who want to be grandparents
- so that you can leave a job
- because you think you're getting too old to wait ('biological clock is ticking').

You also need to ask yourself, will you…
- still be able to have an active social life, go on holiday, or have hobbies?
- want to stay at home and look after your baby?
- mind if having a baby affects your career, if you take a break?
- be able to find childcare and babysitters?
- cope with all the demands of a baby, like lack of sleep, etc?

Babies have a **profound** and **permanent effect** on **parents' lives**. Parents have to adjust their lifestyles and undertake a **lifelong commitment**. Children can be a source of joy and pride, and raising them can bring satisfaction and love to a relationship. Babies that aren't planned are not necessarily unwanted.

Quick Test

1. What influences your sexual role?
2. A stereotypical expectation is that boys will be brave if hurt. **True** or **false**?
3. Is co-habitation socially acceptable?
4. Why might parents apply pressure on you to have a baby?

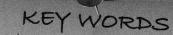

KEY WORDS
Make sure you understand these words before moving on!
- Nature
- Nurture
- Stereotyping
- Culture

Contraception

What is Contraception?

Contraception is the deliberate prevention of pregnancy, by preventing fertilisation or implantation of an egg. The contraception people choose depends on…

- personal preference
- religious belief
- age
- whether a long- or short-term method is needed
- health.

Pregnancy can also be prevented by **sterilisation**. This is done by either cutting or blocking the fallopian (uterine) tube in women, or the sperm tube in men (**vasectomy**).

Emergency contraception is needed after unprotected sex:

- The **morning-after pill** must be taken within 72 hours of unprotected sex. It can be prescribed by a doctor or family planning clinic, or bought from a pharmacist.
- An **IUD** (**intrauterine device**) prevents pregnancy if fitted within 5 days of unprotected sex, by preventing implantation.

Natural Methods

There are three main natural methods of contraception:

1. **NFP** (**natural family planning**) identifies fertile times in the menstrual cycle. It **isn't reliable**, especially if periods are irregular or the woman is ill. Careful daily records must be kept, and intercourse must be avoided during the fertile period. The woman needs to be able to interpret…
   - her cervical mucus
   - her body temperature
   - when she's likely to ovulate.

   Ovulation monitors can be purchased from pharmacists.

2. The **withdrawal method** (coitus interruptus) is when the penis is removed from the vagina before ejaculation. This **isn't reliable** as semen leaks throughout intercourse.

3. **Abstention** from sexual intercourse is saying 'No', and is **100 per cent reliable**.

Quick Test

1. What is contraception?
2. The morning-after pill can only be prescribed by a doctor. **True** or **false**?
3. Which contraceptive method identifies the fertile time in the menstrual cycle?
4. What is another name for the withdrawal method of contraception?

KEY WORDS

Make sure you understand these words before moving on!

- Contraception
- Sterilisation
- Vasectomy

Facts about Contraception

Method	What it Looks Like	% Effective	Advantages	Disadvantages
Male condom		98%	Free from family planning clinics; widely available; protects both parties from STIs (sexually transmitted infections), including AIDS	May split, be damaged, come off, or not be put on correctly
Femidom (female condom)		95%	Protects both partners from STIs, including AIDS	Expensive; penis must enter the condom, not the vagina
Diaphragm (cap) with spermicide (gel or cream)		92–96%	Wide variety available; no health risks from side effects	Must stay in place six hours after intercourse; needs fitting by a doctor and checking regularly
IUD (intrauterine device)		98–99%	Works immediately; can stay in place for 3–10 years	Needs fitting by a doctor; sometimes comes out; may cause heavier, more painful periods
IUS (intrauterine system)		99% +	Works immediately; can stay in place for 5 years; reduces heavy periods	Needs fitting by a doctor; side effects may be acne or tender breasts
Combined pill (contains oestrogen and progestogen), or **Mini pill** (POP) (contains progestogen only)		100%	Easily taken orally	Needs a prescription; unreliable if not taken at the same time each day; vomiting, diarrhoea and antibiotics make it unreliable
Contraceptive implant (slow release progestogen)		99%	Effective for up to 3 years; fertility returns immediately if removed	Can be difficult to remove; may cause irregular or excessive bleeding
Contraceptive injection (progestogen)		99%	Effective for 2–3 months	There's no antidote if the woman changes her mind; fertility may take up to 18 months to return; may cause irregular bleeding

Practice Questions

1 What is the definition of a family?

....

2 Which of the following statements describes a step family? Tick the correct option.

    A Step families are checked by social services.

    B Parents and children live near grandparents.

    C Children live in two households.

    D Step families are formed when one or both people in a couple, with children from a previous relationship, re-marry or co-habit.

3 Which of the following statements are true? Tick the correct options.

    A Adoptive parents must be approved by social services.

    B Residential care homes provide long-term care for children with severe disabilities.

    C A nuclear family includes grandparents.

    D Single-parent families are always mothers and their children.

    E Foster children aren't encouraged to stay in touch with their birth family.

    F Adoptive parents have the same legal rights and responsibilities as birth parents.

    G Foster care is long-term care.

    H Primary socialisation is provided by all families.

4 Fill in the missing words to complete the following sentence.

Sexual roles are decided by .... (your genes) or

.... (the environment you are brought up in).

5 When is emergency contraception needed?

....

6 Choose the correct words from the options given to complete the following sentences.

    not   **natural family planning**   **menstrual cycle**   **infertile**

.... identifies fertile and

.... times in the .... It's

.... reliable.

7 Choose the correct words from the options given to complete the following chart.

IUD   **male condom**   **contraceptive injection**   **contraceptive implant**

diaphragm   **femidom**   **mini pill**

Method of Contraception	What it Looks Like
....	
....	
....	
....	
....	
....	
....	

8 Which of the following statements are true? Tick the correct options.

A   A male condom is 100 per cent effective.

B   A diaphragm protects against STIs, including AIDS.

C   The combined pill is unreliable if taken with some antibiotics.

D   A contraceptive injection can be reversed.

E   The mini pill is taken orally.

F   A contraceptive implant is effective for 3 months.

G   An IUD is effective for 2–3 months.

H   Male condoms are free of charge from family planning clinics.

Male Reproductive System

Seminal vesicle — Bladder — Sperm

Prostate gland — Sperm duct (*vas deferens*)

Sperm — Urethra

Testis — Testis (sperm produced here)

Epididymis (sperm stored here)

Scrotum — Sperm

Penis — Foreskin

Part	Function
Testis	Produces sperm and **testosterone** (hormone).
Scrotum	Bag of skin containing two testes. Hangs outside the body, allowing sperm to be stored at a lower temperature than body heat.
Sperm duct (*vas deferens*)	Sperm travel through this from the testes to the urethra.
Prostate gland and seminal vesicles	Add fluid to the sperm to form **semen**. This activates the sperm and provides energy for it.
Urethra	This tube transports semen and urine out of the body. During intercourse the exit from the bladder is closed, so these two fluids can't mix.
Penis	Varies in length in different males. It's flaccid, but fills with blood, becoming hard when sexually stimulated (erection). It ejaculates semen into the vagina, and then becomes limp.
Foreskin	Covers and protects the end of the penis. It's sometimes surgically removed for medical or religious reasons (circumcision).

Producing and Releasing Sperm

Sperm is **produced by the testes** and **stored** in the **epididymis**. At ejaculation, sperm is released and rushes through the ducts. As it passes along the tube, the **prostate gland** and the **seminal vesicles** release seminal fluid, which nourishes the sperm. The **mixture of sperm and seminal fluid** is a milky white fluid called **semen**.

Female Reproductive System

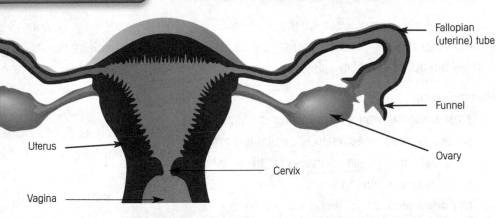

Ovum (egg)

Fallopian (uterine) tube

Funnel

Ovary

Uterus

Cervix

Vagina

Part	Function
Uterus	A pear-shaped organ the size of a clenched fist, with very muscular walls. It increases from approximately 30g in weight to 1kg during pregnancy.
Lining of the uterus (endometrium)	Comes away each month during menstruation (period) if a fertilised ovum (egg) hasn't been implanted in it.
Fallopian tube (uterine tube, oviduct or egg tube)	Links the ovaries with the uterus. Fertilisation takes place here.
Funnel	Catches the released ova and wafts it into the fallopian (uterine) tube.
Ovaries	There are two ovaries, which release ova (eggs) once every 28 days (**ovulation**). They control the levels of oestrogen and progesterone (female sex hormones).
Vagina	10–12 cm long and leads from the outside of the body to the cervix. Sperm are deposited at the top of the vagina during intercourse.
Cervix	A strong ring of muscle at the neck of the uterus, with a small opening to allow menstrual blood and semen to pass through it.

The Menstrual Cycle

The function of the menstrual cycle is to release an egg and prepare the uterus to receive it if it's fertilised.

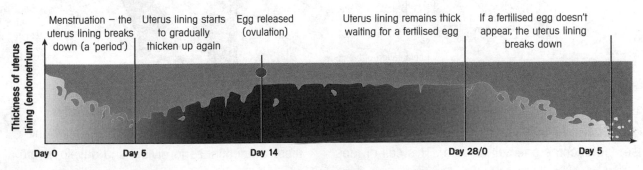

Menstruation – the uterus lining breaks down (a 'period')

Uterus lining starts to gradually thicken up again

Egg released (ovulation)

Uterus lining remains thick waiting for a fertilised egg

If a fertilised egg doesn't appear, the uterus lining breaks down

Thickness of uterus lining (endometrium)

Day 0   Day 5   Day 14   Day 28/0   Day 5

Remember, the cycle can vary enormously from person to person and month to month due to factors such as stress, diet, health, age, etc.

Pre-conceptual Care and Conception

Pre-conceptual Care

For a healthy pregnancy, pre-conceptual care should begin before conception. Pre-conceptual care is based on a healthy lifestyle.

Parents-to-be should…

- **stop smoking**, and avoid passive smoking and smoky atmospheres. Help is available from the NHS (National Health Service) for those who want to stop smoking
- **not drink alcohol**, as it can reduce fertility
- **not take recreational drugs** – support groups can help people to stop
- **check for STIs** (sexually transmitted infections), as certain infections can affect fertility
- **eat a healthy diet**, which is high in fibre, low in sugar, fat and salt, and includes five portions of fruit and vegetables each day
- **exercise** for general fitness and well-being
- **have medical conditions**, e.g. diabetes or epilepsy, **under good control**.

In addition, a mother-to-be should…

- check immunity to rubella and polio from medical records or blood tests
- take a **folic acid** supplement three months before conception to prevent neural tube defects such as Spina Bifida in the baby. **Folate** occurs naturally in foods like leafy green vegetables, nuts and beans. Folic acid is added to fortified breads and cereals.

By leading a healthy lifestyle, couples will maximise their ability to conceive (get pregnant). A mother-to-be is also much more likely to have a safe and successful pregnancy.

Conception

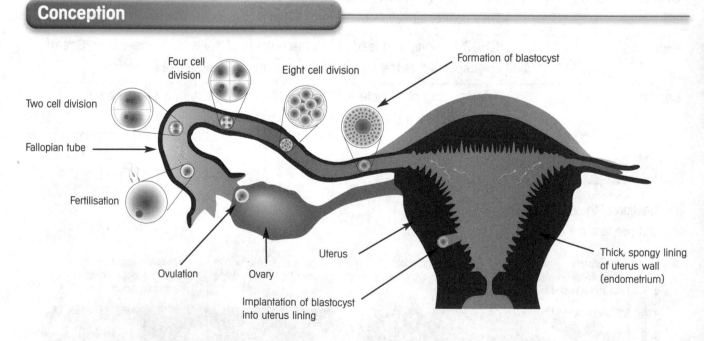

To become pregnant, **fertilisation** of an egg by a single sperm takes place in the fallopian tube. They fuse and become one cell (zygote). This cell divides until it becomes a blastocyst.

If the uterus lining is ready, 4–6 days after fertilisation the blastocyst implants itself in the uterus. It continues to divide, and develops into an embryo.

Genetics

Basic Genetics

There are 46 **chromosomes** in every cell in the body, except for the sex cells, which have 23 each. At conception they become one cell with 46 chromosomes.

These chromosomes are made up of genes, which carry information that determines eye colour, nose shape, etc. **Genes** may be **dominant** (strong) or **recessive** (weak).

Genetic Counselling

Some genes can cause inherited diseases like muscular dystrophy and cystic fibrosis.

Genetic conditions like Down's Syndrome are caused by incorrect gene make-up.

Genetic counselling is offered if…
- there is a family history of inherited disease, or a previous child has an inherited disease
- a couple are closely related
- the mother has two or more miscarriages
- ante-natal screening shows an abnormal result.

Inheritance of Sex

Gender (in mammals) is determined by **sex chromosomes**:
- XX = female. All **egg cells** carry X chromosomes.
- XY = male. Half the **sperm cells** carry X chromosomes and half carry Y chromosomes.

The sex of an individual depends on whether the egg is **fertilised** by an X-carrying sperm or a Y-carrying sperm:
- An egg fertilised by an X sperm will become a girl (X from egg and X from sperm = XX).
- An egg fertilised by a Y sperm will become a boy (X from egg and Y from sperm = XY).

The **chances** of an egg being fertilised by an X-carrying sperm or a Y-carrying sperm are equal, so there are approximately equal numbers of male and female offspring.

Male   Female

Female   Male

Quick Test

1. What is semen a mixture of?
2. Where are eggs stored?
3. The quality of eggs deteriorates with age. **True** or **false**?
4. Where does a fertilised egg implant itself?
5. Is the sex of a baby determined by an egg or a sperm?

KEY WORDS
Make sure you understand these words before moving on!
- Testosterone
- Semen
- Ovulation
- Folic acid
- Fertilisation
- Chromosomes
- Genetic counselling

Early Stages of Pregnancy

Confirming Pregnancy

Possible signs of pregnancy are...

- a missed period
- more frequent urination
- feeling exhausted, dizzy or faint
- enlarged, tender breasts

- nipples and areola changing colour
- a metallic taste in the mouth
- a sudden dislike to certain smells and tastes
- sickness or nausea (may be in the morning, but can be all day).

Pregnancy Testing

Pregnancy tests may be carried out at home or done by a GP or at a pharmacy. They can be used from the day a period is due, or earlier.

To take a pregnancy test, place an absorbent sampler in a mid-stream urine sample, to detect the presence of the hormone human chorionic gonadotrophin (HCG). The result is shown in a window on the test stick.

Tests are accurate, but instructions must be carefully followed to avoid a false, negative result.

Estimated Delivery Date

The average length of pregnancy is 37–42 weeks. Only 5 per cent of babies arrive on the due date.

To calculate the **estimated delivery date** (EDD), to the last day of the period...

- add 9 months and 7 days, *or*
- count 280 days.

An early dating scan will give you a reliable indication of the EDD.

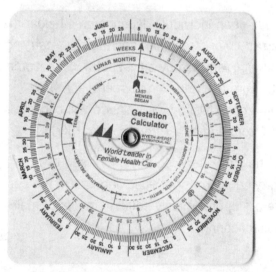

Losses in Pregnancy

Miscarriage is the loss of pregnancy before 24 weeks. Up to 80 per cent of miscarriages happen in the first 12 weeks. After 24 weeks, the baby is **viable** (able to survive).

An **abortion** is the medical process of ending a pregnancy before 24 weeks so it doesn't result in the birth of a baby.

A baby born dead after 24 weeks is a **stillborn** baby.

An **ectopic pregnancy** happens if a fertilised egg implants itself somewhere other than the uterus, e.g. in the fallopian tube. It can be dangerous for the mother.

Multiple Pregnancies

Multiple Pregnancies

Multiple pregnancies take place when more than one foetus develops in the uterus. They can occur naturally, but are more likely to take place if fertility treatment is used.

The terms used to describe multiple birth children are...

- **twins** for **two babies**
- **triplets** for **three babies**
- **quadruplets** for **four babies**
- **quintuplets** for **five babies**
- **sextuplets** for **six babies**.

Twins

If a fertilised egg **splits completely** into two parts, each part develops into an identical baby.

Identical (monozygotic) twins...

- have identical genes
- look the same
- have the same blood group
- are the same sex
- share a placenta.

If a fertilised egg **splits only partially** into two, then **conjoined twins** result. This is very rare.

If two eggs are released at the same time, and fertilised by two separate sperm, then two babies will result.

Non-identical (dizygotic or fraternal) twins...

- have their own placenta
- don't look alike
- can be different sexes
- have different genes.

Possible Complications

Possible complications with multiple pregnancies are...

- low birth weight
- premature labour
- the need for a Caesarean section
- more risks to the mother's health.

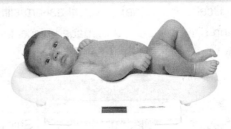

Quick Test

1. An early sign of pregnancy is weight gain. **True** or **false**?
2. At what age do babies become viable?
3. What do the letters EDD stand for?
4. What is the average length of a pregnancy in weeks?
5. Which kind of twin shares a placenta?

KEY WORDS
Make sure you understand these words before moving on!
- Estimated delivery date
- Viable
- Monozygotic
- Conjoined
- Fraternal

A Healthy, Comfortable Pregnancy

What to Do

To have a healthy, comfortable pregnancy…

- eat healthily, including foods high in NSP (non-starch polysaccharide – fibre). This helps to avoid constipation, which can be a problem in pregnancy
- exercise
- rest and relax
- choose machine washable clothing that isn't tight around the bump, and allows room for growth. Stretchy lightweight fabrics are good
- choose supportive, adjustable, wide-strapped bras
- avoid high-heeled shoes
- have regular dental check-ups.

What to Avoid

To have a healthy, comfortable pregnancy, you should avoid…

- **alcohol** – this can cause FAS (foetal alcohol syndrome), stillbirth, a small baby / baby with a low birth weight, a baby with a small head / facial abnormality
- **drugs** – these can cause low birth weight, withdrawal symptoms in the baby, an irritable baby with a high-pitched cry, mental impairment
- **smoking** – nicotine and carbon dioxide increase the risk of having a premature baby, and can cause low birth weight, miscarriage, stillbirth, SIDS (Sudden Infant Death Syndrome), physical abnormalities, learning difficulties, and a damaged placenta
- **some foods** – see below.

Foods to Avoid	Problem	Effect
Eggs, unless hard-boiled; products containing raw egg	Salmonella	Food poisoning
Unpasteurised milk / milk products, e.g. soft cheese; incorrectly reheated cook-chill food; undercooked meat; pâté	Listeriosis	Can cause miscarriage, still birth, severe illness
Liver and liver products	Vitamin A	Too much harms the baby
Fruit and vegetables with soil on; undercooked meat	Toxoplasmosis	Miscarriage, still birth, blind baby
Coffee and products containing caffeine	Caffeine	Miscarriage and low birth weight; possible links to autism and ADHD (attention deficit hyperactivity disorder)
Peanuts and peanut products	May cause allergies	Eczema, asthma and hayfever

Causes of Infertility

Infertility (the inability to conceive) affects both sexes, and one in ten couples.

Medical technology helps many of those affected, either through the NHS or private sector.

Cause	Problem
Blocked fallopian tube / thick cervical mucus	Sperm can't reach the egg
No ovulation / hormone imbalance	No egg
Insufficient sperm / poor quality	Egg won't be fertilised

Assisted Conception

Gynaecologists have specialist knowledge of the functions and diseases of the female reproductive system. They treat problems like infertility.

There are a number of ways to assist conception:

- In **IVF** (*in vitro* **fertilisation**) you first have hormone treatment to stimulate ovulation. Then eggs are surgically removed and penetrated by sperm in a 'test tube'. At 8 cell division, they're placed into either the uterus or fallopian tube.
- **Egg donation** involves eggs being collected from donors, and IVF procedures are then used.
- In **donor insemination** donated sperm is placed directly into the uterus or used in an IVF procedure.
- The partner's sperm is placed directly into the uterus.
- **ICSI** (**intra-cytoplasmic sperm injection**) is when an individual sperm is injected directly into the egg.
- **Surrogacy** is where another woman has a baby for a couple who can't have a child themselves.
- **PGD** (**pre-implementation Genetic Diagnosis**) is used by couples who have been identified as being carriers of a serious genetic disorder. Embryos are screened after treatment, and only those that are healthy are used.

Quick Test

1. What sort of straps should a bra worn in pregnancy have?
2. What causes FAS?
3. Infertility only affects women. **True** or **false**?
4. Which professional treats infertility in women?
5. What do the letters IVF stand for?
6. What do the letters ICSI stand for?

KEY WORDS

Make sure you understand these words before moving on!
- IVF
- Egg donation
- Donor insemination
- Surrogacy

Development of Unborn Child

Length of Pregnancy

Pregnancy is divided into **three trimesters**:
1–3 months, **4–6 months**, and **7–9 months**.

Weeks 6 to 12

At **week 6**… • there is initial development of legs, brain, spine, internal organs, blood, bone, muscles, ears and eyes • the **embryo**'s heart is beating.	Actual size
At **week 8**… • the **foetus** looks more human • the arms, legs, shoulders, ears and eyes can be seen • the foetus moves in the amniotic sac • the heartbeat is visible on a scan.	Actual size
At **week 12**, the foetus… • is fully formed • swims by kicking • can swallow, clench a fist, hiccup, suck its thumb • has well-developed sex organs • is sensitive to heat, light and sound • has its eyes closed.	Actual size

Weeks 24 to 36

At **week 24**, the foetus…
• weighs approximately 700g (1.5 lb)
• has hair, wrinkled skin, fingernails and fingerprints
• is covered in vernix (a white, greasy substance, which protects the skin and keeps it waterproof) and lanugo (fine hair that keeps it warm)
• is active, with definite periods of waking and sleeping.

After 24 weeks, the baby grows and gets stronger. If it was born now it would be **viable** (have a reasonable chance of surviving). This is because its development, except for the lungs, is complete. If it was born now it would need special care in a neonatal intensive care unit (NICU) or special care baby unit (SCBU).

By **32–36 weeks**, the baby is usually lying head downwards. This is called the **cephalic** position.

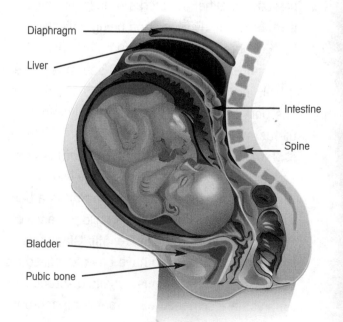

Diaphragm

Liver

Intestine

Spine

Bladder

Pubic bone

Development of Unborn Child

Placenta

The placenta, umbilical cord and amniotic sac are produced by the fertilised egg.

The **placenta**…

- is the only disposable organ in the body
- is attached to the wall of the uterus and is expelled after birth as the afterbirth
- grows to 2.5cm thick, 15cm across, and weighs 500g.

The placenta maintains and nourishes the baby by letting oxygen, carbon dioxide, amino fats, vitamins and minerals pass from the mother's blood. Waste products from the growing baby pass through the placenta to the mother. Their blood doesn't mix.

Alcohol, nicotine, viruses, drugs and antibodies pass to the baby through the placenta.

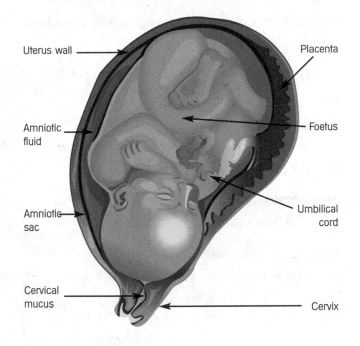

Amniotic Sac and Umbilical Cord

The **amniotic sac** is filled with amniotic fluid, which keeps the baby's temperature at 37°C. It also cushions and protects the baby from bangs.

The **umbilical cord**…

- is approximately 50cm long and 2cm wide
- contains three blood vessels, which carry blood between the mother and baby
- is cut and clamped after birth.

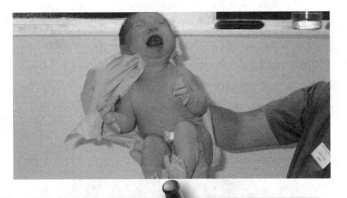

Quick Test

1. When is the baby fully formed?
2. A baby born after 24 weeks can't survive. **True** or **false**?
3. How are the placenta, umbilical cord and amniotic sac made?
4. The mother's antibodies can pass to the baby. **True** or **false**?
5. What is the amniotic sac filled with?

KEY WORDS

Make sure you understand these words before moving on!

- Foetus
- Cephalic
- Placenta
- Amniotic sac
- Umbilical cord

Ante-natal Tests and Scans

Tests and Checks

Routine tests during pregnancy detect any problems with mother and baby.

The **abdomen** is **palpated** to check size, position and movement of the foetus.

The **legs** are checked for…
- swelling, which may indicate pre-eclampsia
- varicose veins.

Blood pressure is checked, because high blood pressure may indicate pre-eclampsia.

Urine is also checked regularly.

Urine Check For...	Presence May Indicate...
Protein (albumen)	Pre-eclampsia, bladder / kidney infections
Ketones	Ill health / dehydration

Chlamydia can also be detected using a urine test.

Other symptoms of **pre-eclampsia** are **blurred vision, headaches, upper abdominal pain** and **swollen fingers and ankles**. Pre-eclampsia is managed by hospital admission, medication, close monitoring and possible early delivery, to avoid eclampsia.

Eclampsia is a serious condition, which may lead to convulsions, multiple organ failure, and death of mother and baby.

The **foetal heartbeat** is checked for its presence and rate using a sonic aid or pinard stethoscope.

Blood tests are taken to check for…
- the mother's blood group, and the rhesus factor
- rubella immunity
- Hepatitis B
- anaemia
- thalassaemia
- sickle-cell anaemia
- HIV.

Taking Blood Pressure

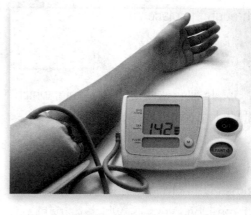

Scans

Ultrasound scans can be 2D, 3D or 4D. A hand held scanner over the abdomen, which is covered in gel, reflects sound waves, which project an image of the baby and its internal organs onto a screen.

Scanning…
- confirms pregnancy
- gives exact foetal age and size
- checks the number of foetuses
- checks for abnormalities, e.g. limbs and internal organs
- checks heartbeat
- checks the umbilical cord
- checks the position of the placenta.

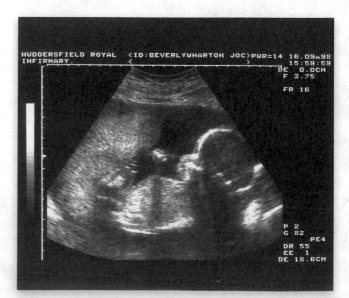

Tests During Pregnancy

Screening Tests

The two main screening tests are...
- nuchal fold translucency
- triple / quadruple test (serum screening).

In the **nuchal fold translucency test**, an ultrasound scan looks at the fold of skin on the back of the baby's neck, and the fluid found there is measured. Excess fluid could indicate Down's syndrome.

Blood screening is only accurate in single pregnancies that have been accurately dated with an early scan.

The **triple / quadruple test** is a blood test, which measures the level of two hormones: HCG and oestriol, and AFP (alphafetoprotein).

These measurements, used with a woman's age, estimate the possibility of genetic conditions, e.g. Down's syndrome. High levels of AFP indicate an increased risk of Spina Bifida.

If screening tests show an increased risk of abnormality, diagnostic tests can be done to confirm the findings.

Diagnostic Tests

The two main invasive diagnostic tests are...
- amniocentesis
- chorionic villus sampling (CVS).

An **amniocentesis** test is normally done at 15–19 weeks of pregnancy. A sample of amniotic fluid is removed using an ultrasound scan, and a hollow needle inserted into the uterus. The fluid is examined to detect...
- genetic conditions such as Down's syndrome or Edwards' syndrome
- Spina Bifida
- the sex of the baby
- viral infections
- the baby's lung development.

Amniocentesis is also offered if there's a family history of chromosomal abnormality, or if the mother has had a previous Down's syndrome pregnancy.

In chorionic villus sampling (**CVS**) a sample of placenta tissue is removed using a hollow needle and ultrasound scan. It detects the same conditions as amniocentesis, but has a higher risk of causing miscarriage.

Quick Test

1. What could high blood pressure during pregnancy indicate?
2. An ultrasound scan uses microwaves. **True** or **false**?
3. What could excess fluid on the back of a baby's neck indicate?

KEY WORDS

Make sure you understand these words before moving on!
- Eclampsia
- Scans
- Nuchal fold translucency test
- Triple / quadruple test
- Amniocentesis
- CVS

Health Care for Mum and Baby

Midwives

A **midwife** has specialised training in the care of women before, during and after pregnancy.

Midwives...
- conduct the booking-in visit
- carry out routine testing
- arrange specialist tests and scans
- run ante-natal classes
- may administer some drugs
- deliver babies in straightforward births
- advise on caring for the newborn baby, e.g. breastfeeding, bathing.

You can be a...
- **community midwife**
- **hospital midwife**, *or*
- **independent midwife**.

Community midwives work as part of a team. They provide ante-natal clinic care in normal pregnancies and carry out post-natal visits in the woman's home. They also attend home births.

Hospital midwives work on the labour ward and help women in labour and during birth. They also work in ante-natal and post-natal wards.

Independent midwives don't work for the NHS, are paid for by the woman, and attend home births.

Medical Practitioners

A **general practitioner** (**GP**) may sometimes share care, with the midwife, for the mother during pregnancy and post-natally. GPs conduct the post-natal examination six weeks after birth.

An **obstetrician** is a specialist, based in a hospital, who cares for women with complications during pregnancy, labour and birth. Only women with a problem will see an obstetrician.

Hand Held Notes

Hand held notes are kept by the mother and brought to all her ante-natal appointments. The notes include...
- name, address and contact number, ethnic origin, next of kin
- general health and family history
- history of previous pregnancies and labours
- ante-natal assessments, including all tests
- health issues relating to pregnancy
- estimated delivery date (EDD)
- growth charts of the baby
- the birth plan.

The **advantages** of **hand held notes** are that they are accessible, all information is stored in one place, and they can be invaluable in an emergency.

Some of the information in the notes is also stored by the mother's hospital, GP and midwife, and can be accessed by computer.

Hand Held Notes

Ante-natal Classes

In the last eight weeks of pregnancy, mothers-to-be can attend ante-natal classes at their local hospital or clinic. These provide useful advice on childbirth and childcare, and are run by midwives.

They are an excellent way to meet other mums and mums-to-be, and get valuable information. Most classes are also suitable for fathers-to-be.

The Role of the Father

A father-to-be has an important role to play, and can help and support his partner.

During pregnancy, a father-to-be can…
- attend all scans and appointments
- read up on pregnancy and childbirth
- go to ante-natal classes
- provide emotional support
- offer practical help, e.g. with housework.

During labour, he can…
- be present at the birth
- offer reassurance and practical help, e.g. rubbing back
- let the midwife know his partner's wishes.

The **birth partner** may not be the father, but someone chosen by the mother to provide support.

Birth Plan

Women are encouraged to think about their ideas and expectations of birth. They can write these down in a **birth plan**.

A birth plan includes the following:
- place of birth
- who will be present
- type of pain relief and birth position that you prefer
- whether to have an oxytocin injection to help deliver the placenta
- views on episiotomy, forceps and Ventouse delivery
- how to monitor labour
- personal requirements, e.g. student present, what (if any) music to play
- religious and dietary requirements
- who will cut the umbilical cord
- whether Vitamin K will be given to the baby
- what happens to the baby afterwards, i.e. baby placed skin to skin with the mum at birth.

A woman's wishes will always be taken into consideration, but it may not always be possible for her to have the exact birth that she planned.

Quick Test

1. Which professional does the booking-in visit?
2. Health visitors deliver babies. **True** or **false**?
3. Who keeps the hand held notes in pregnancy?
4. Is it always possible to follow a birth plan?
5. Which specialist cares for women during pregnancy, labour and birth?

KEY WORDS

Make sure you understand these words before moving on!
- Midwife
- GP
- Obstetrician
- Hand held notes
- Birth plan

Practice Questions

1 Which of the following is part of the female reproductive system? Tick the correct option.

    A   Urethra ☐

    B   Cervix ☐

    C   Scrotum ☐

    D   Foreskin ☐

2 Choose the correct words from the options given to complete the following sentences.

epididymis	uterus	vagina	cervix
testes	ovaries	penis	sperm

    a) Eggs are released from the _____ .

    b) The scrotum contains two _____ .

    c) The _____ is found at the neck of the uterus.

    d) The _____ ejaculates semen.

    e) Sperm are deposited at the top of the _____ .

    f) The _____ is a pear shaped organ.

    g) Semen is a mixture of seminal fluid and _____ .

    h) Sperm is stored in the _____ .

3 When should pre-conceptual care begin?

_____

4 Fill in the missing words to complete the following sentences.

If a _____ egg splits completely into _____ parts, each develops

into an _____ twin.

5 During pregnancy, which of the following is urine checked for? Tick the correct options.

    A   Protein ☐   **E**   Chlamydia ☐

    B   Anaemia ☐   **F**   Ketones ☐

    C   Rubella ☐   **G**   Rhesus factor ☐

    D   Hepatitis B ☐

6 Choose the correct words from the options given to complete the following chart.

nuchal fold translucency   triple test   amniocentesis   blood test

Test	What it Does
....	Measures AFP
....	Detects the baby's sex
....	Measures fluid on the back of the neck
....	Checks for anaemia

7 Explain how a scanner works.

....

....

8 Which of the following statements about amniocentesis is true? Tick the correct option.

A A sample of placenta tissue is removed. ◯

B The fluid at the back of the neck is removed. ◯

C It's offered if the mother has had a previous Down's syndrome pregnancy. ◯

D The amount of AFP is measured. ◯

9 What **three** things can a father do to help his partner during labour?

i) ....

ii) ....

iii) ....

Home Births

Home Births

The **advantages** of a **home birth** are…
- the familiar surroundings make the mother relaxed
- the midwife is more likely to be known
- privacy is guaranteed
- there's no routine to follow, e.g. mealtimes
- no transport is needed
- more people can be present at the birth
- there are no other babies crying to disturb the mother
- it causes less disruption to other children in the family.

A **home birth** is **advised against** if…
- it's a multiple birth
- labour is premature (before 37 weeks)
- the mother has had a previous Caesarean section
- there are medical problems, e.g. high blood pressure, diabetes
- home conditions are unsuitable
- the mother is over 35 or under 17, depending on individual circumstances
- the baby is in an unsuitable position
- it's a first, fourth or subsequent baby
- there's been a previous post partum haemorrhage.

Preparing for a Home Birth

Before a home birth, the midwife advises about…
- the room for the birth, because the temperature needs to be controlled and the room must be big enough
- how the baby will be born, e.g. on a bed, beanbag
- protective materials to use on the bed and carpets
- using a birthing pool: filling it and maintaining its temperature
- hand washing facilities that the midwife will need.

About one month before the birth, the midwife delivers a sealed sterile **birth pack** to the home. It contains cotton drapes, sterile cord clamps, scissors, etc.

When attending the birth, the midwife brings the necessary drugs and oxygen, in case the baby needs resuscitating.

Advantages of Hospital Births

Advantages of a **hospital birth** are that…

- equipment is available for emergency use, e.g. if a Caesarean section is needed, or an incubator
- equipment is available for foetal monitoring, e.g. cardio-tacograph, scanner
- midwives are always available
- there are other mothers to share experiences with
- visiting is restricted, so the mother can rest
- the mother doesn't have to cook, clean or look after other children
- epidural anaesthetic is available.

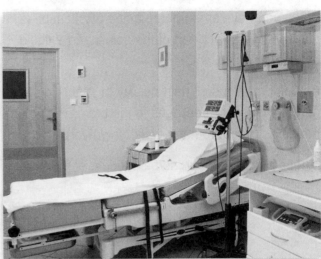

Home-from-home Suites

Some hospitals have **home-from-home suites**, which are designed to look like hotel rooms. They can help to make the mother relax. They may have a kitchenette, birthing pool and an en-suite bathroom. Some have double beds so the father can stay and share the first few hours after birth.

Disadvantages of home-from-home suites are that they…

- can't be booked in advance
- are only suitable for low risk, normal births, e.g. if epidural or Ventouse extraction isn't needed.

Domino Delivery Scheme

In the **Domino Delivery Scheme**, a community midwife accompanies the mother to hospital and delivers the baby.

If there are no complications, the midwife returns home with mother and baby six hours later.

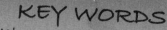

Quick Test

1. Before a home birth, what does the midwife deliver?
2. At the time of a home birth, what will the midwife bring?
3. Hospital births are advised for multiple pregnancies. **True** or **false**?
4. A hospital has equipment ready for emergencies. **True** or **false**?

KEY WORDS
Make sure you understand these words before moving on!
- Home birth
- Birth pack
- Hospital birth

Pain Relief Drugs in Labour

Epidural Anaesthetic

When you have an **epidural**, a fine plastic tube is placed in the lower part of the spine, and a liquid anaesthetic is put into this.

An epidural stops all pain quickly by blocking the nerves that send messages to the brain. The mother is numb from the waist downwards.

Mobile epidurals allow some freedom of movement.

Disadvantages of epidurals are that...
- they must be administered by an anaesthetist, so they can only be given in hospital
- the mother often doesn't know when to 'push' (because she can't feel the contractions)
- they may cause headaches and backache after birth
- they may increase the length of labour and the need for forceps or Ventouse delivery
- they take time to be effective
- the mother may need a catheter, as she's unable to feel when her bladder is full
- the mother may need a fluids drip.

Pethidine

Pethidine is a drug that is injected into a deep muscle in the leg or bottom to relieve pain.

Disadvantages of pethidine are that...
- the baby may be born drowsy and slower to breathe, as the drug crosses the placenta
- the mother can feel disoriented and that she lacks control
- it takes about 20 minutes to take effect.

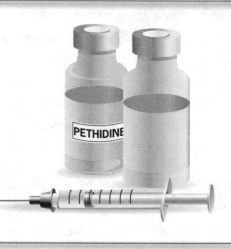

Entonox (Gas and Air)

Entonox is a mixture of nitrous oxide and oxygen. It's inhaled through a mouthpiece or mask, which is controlled by the mother. It isn't harmful to the baby.

Disadvantages of entonox are that...
- it must be used as soon as any discomfort from a contraction is felt, because it takes 15 seconds to have any effect and 35 seconds to get maximum relief
- the effect wears off quickly
- the pain isn't completely removed
- the mother may feel sick
- the mother may have a dry mouth.

Alternatives to Drugs in Labour

TENS Machine

A **TENS** (Transcutaneous Electrical Nerve Stimulation) machine has four flat pads containing electrodes, which are attached to the mother's back. When she feels pain she sends electrical impulses to her back through a hand held control. This releases endorphins, which block out pain messages going to the brain.

TENS machines may be available in hospitals. They can also be hired or bought, and have no side effects.

Disadvantages of TENS machines are that…
- they can't be used in water births
- the mother can't shower or bathe during labour
- they don't work if pain is intense – they're most effective in Stage 1 of labour.

Water Birth

A **water birth** takes place in a birthing pool, which looks like a large bath or paddling pool. The water is kept at a constant temperature of 37°C. Birthing pools can be hired or bought for home births.

Disadvantages of water births are that they…
- can be difficult to set up, and to maintain the correct water temperature at home
- can't be used with pethidine or epidurals
- are only suitable for normal, low risk pregnancies.

Other Kinds of Pain Relief

Other kinds of pain relief are…
- controlled breathing and massage
- acupuncture
- homeopathy
- aromatherapy
- reflexology.

Disadvantages of these kinds of pain relief are that…
- they may not be effective
- information and training is needed from qualified people.

Quick Test

1. What kind of pain relief must be given by an anaesthetist?
2. Name the drug given as an injection for pain relief.
3. Entonox gives 100 percent pain relief. **True** or **false**?
4. Can TENS machines be used in water births?
5. At what temperature should the water in a birthing pool be kept?

KEY WORDS

Make sure you understand these words before moving on!
- Epidural
- Pethidine
- Entonox
- TENS
- Water birth

Labour

What is Labour?

Labour is the **process of giving birth**, which is started by hormones.

The mother has to work hard so that the contractions of the uterus can open the cervix, and the baby can be pushed out.

Labour lasts from approximately 1 to 24 hours.

There are **three stages** in **labour**.

Stage 1 of Labour

In **Stage 1** of **labour**, the muscles in the uterus gradually open up (dilate) the cervix to 8–10 cm. This is wide enough for the baby's head to pass through.

Signs that labour has started appear in any order and include…
- a **show**
- **contractions**
- waters breaking
- backache, nausea, vomiting and diarrhoea.

When you have a **show**, the plug of mucus sealing the cervix comes away. It may be bloodstained. This may be unnoticed by the mother.

Labour contractions are **weak** and **irregular to start with**. They **gradually become stronger**, **more intense** and **closer together**. The uterus becomes tight for up to a minute, and then relaxes. As contractions get stronger and closer together, they cause pain.

Braxton Hicks contractions can be felt after 32 weeks. These are only 'practice' contractions, and are eratic and uncomfortable rather than painful.

When your **waters break** (rupturing of the membranes), the amniotic fluid should be clear or slightly pink, and leaking out of the vagina. The fluid may come in a slow trickle or a sudden gush. The presence of meconium in the fluid can indicate a distressed baby. Sometimes the waters don't break until the second stage of labour.

Backache, **nausea**, **vomiting** and **diarrhoea** are common in the first stage of labour.

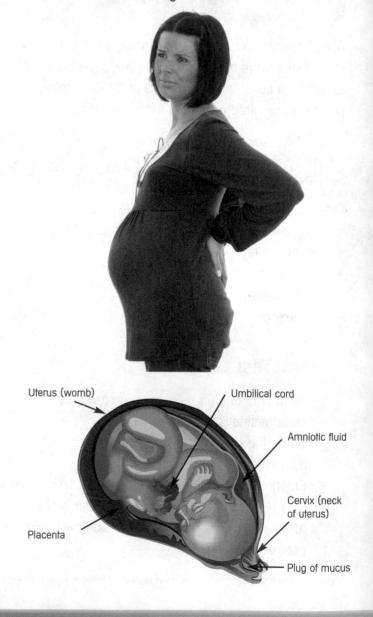

Uterus (womb)

Umbilical cord

Amniotic fluid

Cervix (neck of uterus)

Placenta

Plug of mucus

Stage 2 of Labour

In **Stage 2** of **labour**, the following takes place:

1. Very strong contractions push the baby along the **birth canal** (which is formed by the uterus, cervix and vagina).

2. The mother has an urge to 'push'.

3. The midwife gives guidance so that the head is born gradually. When the widest part of the head comes out of the vagina, it is known as **crowning**.

4. Sometimes the head causes a small tear, which may or may not be stitched.

5. Sometimes an **episiotomy** (a cut in the vagina) is needed to let the head pass through. This is stitched.

6. After the head emerges, the body slides out quickly and easily.

7. The baby may cry and breathe as the head emerges, or after the shoulders and body are pushed out.

8. The umbilical cord Is cut between two clamps. This doesn't hurt the baby.

9. The baby is a separate person.

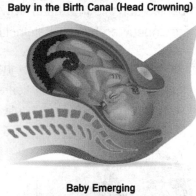

Baby in the Birth Canal (Head Crowning)

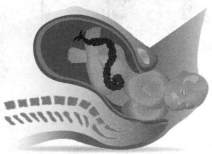

Baby Emerging

Baby is a Separate Person

Stage 3 of Labour

In **Stage 3** of **labour**, an injection of **oxytocin** may be given to the mother to stop excessive bleeding, and help the placenta and remaining cord to be delivered quickly. This takes 5–15 minutes.

Alternatively, the woman may have a physiological third stage, where the placenta is left attached to the baby until it's delivered. Breastfeeding helps the placenta to detach and deliver quickly.

Then the placenta is examined, and labour is complete. Any necessary stitching or repair is done.

Birth Complications

Position of the Baby

Sometimes babies don't lie in a head-down position and can't be manoeuvred by an obstetrician into it.

The **breech position** is when either the baby's legs or bottom are first. A Caesarean section might be advised.	In the **transverse position**, the baby lies across the uterus and must be delivered by Caesarean section.	In the **oblique position**, the baby lies at an angle in the uterus, and must be delivered by Caesarean section.

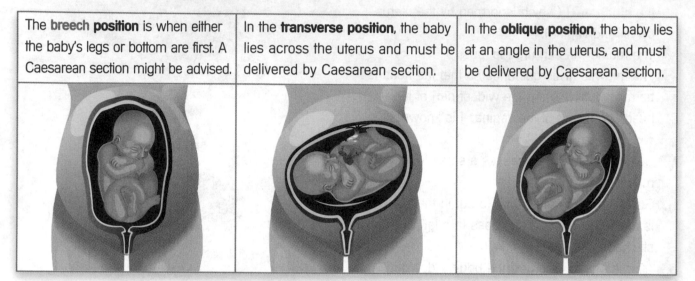

Induction

Labour is 'induced' (artificially started) if...
- the baby is overdue (term + 12 days)
- the mother has pre-eclampsia, eclampsia or diabetes
- the baby is failing to grow (the placenta isn't working properly).

It can take several days to establish labour. A combination of the following methods may be used during **induction**:
- sweeping or artificial rupturing of the membranes
- prostaglandin pessary
- intravenous drip of the hormone oxytocin (syntocinon).

Assisted Delivery

Assisted delivery may be necessary if...
- the baby is in distress
- the mother is unable to push the baby out.

A **Ventouse delivery** is when a metal or plastic cup is attached to the baby's head by a vacuum. The baby is eased out when contractions occur.

A **forceps delivery** takes place when forceps (curved metal blades) are applied to either side of the baby's head. The baby is eased out when contractions occur.

Ventouse Delivery

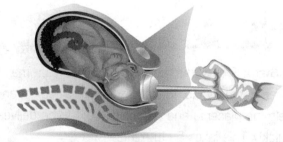

Forceps Delivery

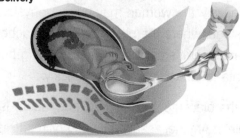

What is a Caesarean Section?

A **Caesarean section** is an operation that cuts open the abdominal wall and uterus along the bikini line, so the baby can be removed.

After the baby is removed, two clamps are put on the umbilical cord and the cord is cut between the two clamps. The placenta is removed. The uterus and abdomen are stitched.

The mother takes up to six weeks to recover.

There are two kinds of Caesarean section:
- elective
- emergency.

Elective Caesarean	Emergency Caesarean
A date 2–3 weeks before the estimated delivery date is chosen for an **elective Caesarean**, before labour starts naturally. A spinal anaesthetic is used so that the mother remains awake and can hold her baby immediately after birth. Reasons for an elective Caesarean are when… • the baby is in the wrong position • the mother is HIV positive • the placenta is blocking the entrance to the birth canal • it's a multiple birth • the mother has had previous Caesarean section(s).	For an **emergency Caesarean**, a general anaesthetic is sometimes used due to lack of time, so the mother will be unconscious during delivery. Reasons for an emergency Caesarean are… • foetal distress, shown by the baby passing meconium or having a prolonged increased / decreased heartbeat • eclampsia or severe pre-eclampsia • severe bleeding from the uterus • progress in labour has stopped • undiagnosed breech position.

Quick Test

1. Which organs form the birth canal?
2. The umbilical cord is cut between two clamps. **True** or **false**?
3. What is the name for artificially starting labour?
4. A Ventouse delivery pulls the baby out. **True** or **false**?
5. How long does recovery take after a Caesarean section?

KEY WORDS
Make sure you understand these words before moving on!
- Show
- Contractions
- Braxton Hicks
- Birth canal
- Crowning
- Oxytocin
- Breech
- Induction
- Ventouse
- Forceps
- Caesarean section

Special Care for Babies

SCBUs and NICUs

SCBUs (special care baby units) and **NICUs** (neonatal intensive care units) look after some babies after they're born.

The units are staffed by neonatologists, doctors, specially trained nurses and midwives.

At first a baby may be cared for on a one-to-one basis.

The level of care decreases as their health improves. Some babies spend only a few hours in a SCBU, others several months.

Which Babies Need Special Care?

Special care may be needed by babies who...
- are premature
- have medical problems, e.g. breathing difficulties
- are born to diabetic or drug-addicted mothers
- are shocked after a difficult delivery.

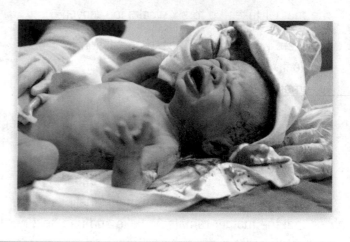

Specialist Equipment in a SCBU

There is a range of specialist equipment in a SCBU.

An **incubator**...
- helps breathing by filtering and humidifying air
- keeps babies warm and isolated from infection
- has portholes, so attention can be given easily.

Light therapy is placed above an incubator to treat jaundice (babies' eyes must be protected from ultra-violet rays). **Jaundice** is **caused by high levels** of **bilirubin**, which can cause brain damage.

A **ventilator** helps babies to breathe. It provides oxygen (at a controlled level to avoid brain damage).

A **nasogastric tube**...
- feeds the mother's expressed breast milk or formula milk directly into the stomach through a tube in the nose
- is used if babies don't have a mature sucking / swallowing reflex, or use too much energy feeding.

An **intravenous line** passes fluids and drugs into babies. Babies are fed nutrients through an intravenous line if they're unable to digest milk.

A **monitor**...
- checks breathing, heartbeat and oxygen concentration
- is placed on babies' skin, and linked to screens and alarms.

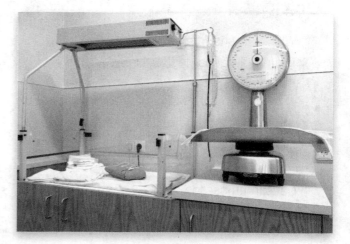

Premature Babies

Premature babies are born **before full term** (i.e. before 37 weeks). They weigh less than 2.5kg / 5lbs at birth. The earlier a baby arrives the more likely it is to need medical help, and have developmental delay in later life.

Characteristics of premature babies are...
- underdeveloped lungs / breathing difficulties
- the inability to suck and swallow
- the inability to regulate body temperature
- small size
- low birth weight and little body fat
- a weak immune system
- low calcium, iron and blood sugar levels
- red, wrinkled skin
- a large head.

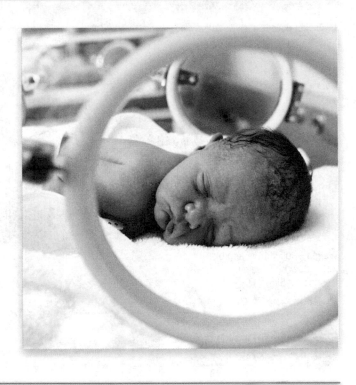

Bonding

Bonding is the **feelings of love and affection between a parent and child**.

This can be difficult with premature babies because the parents...
- may feel the baby doesn't belong to them, it belongs to the hospital
- may be afraid to love the baby in case it dies.

There are ways in which bonding can be encouraged for all babies.

Parents can...
- provide physical care, e.g. nappy changing, washing, feeding
- talk and sing to their baby, making eye contact
- have skin-to-skin contact by stroking and cuddling ('kangaroo' cuddling for premature babies)
- provide toys and clothes.

The mother can also put the baby to the breast. Even if the baby can't feed, the contact will help establish the mother's milk supply.

Quick Test

1. Where are premature babies looked after?
2. A SCBU only looks after premature babies. **True** or **false**?
3. Which equipment in a SCBU keeps babies warm?
4. Parents shouldn't touch premature babies. **True** or **false**?

KEY WORDS
Make sure you understand these words before moving on!
- SCBUs
- NICUs
- Incubator
- Premature babies

Newborn Babies

Physical Characteristics

Umbilical cord – after 7–10 days it shrivels and drops off

Skin – may have milia (small white / yellow spots), vernix, lanugo and birthmarks

Eyes – newborn white-skinned babies have blue / grey eyes; dark-skinned babies have brown eyes

Fontanelles – tough membranes that protect the brain until the skull bones join together

Weight – full term is approx. 3.5kg (low birth weight is less than 2.5kg)

Comparatively large head, large tummy, short legs

Length – average of 50cm

Reflex Actions and Senses

Reflex actions are **present at birth** and include…

- sucking and swallowing
- rooting
- walking / stepping
- falling (Moro)
- the grasp reflex
- the startle reflex
- crawling
- blinking
- asymmetric tonic neck.

Newborn babies make use of all five **senses**:

- **Smell** – they recognise the smell of their mother's milk, and dislike unpleasant smells.
- **Taste** – they show dislike for some tastes.
- **Sight** – they focus best at a 20cm distance, and react to bright lights.
- **Hearing** – they respond to sound, and recognise their mother's voice.
- **Touch** – they can feel pain, and are comforted by skin-to-skin contact and cuddles.

Apgar Test

At 1–5 minutes after birth, the condition of newborn babies is checked using the **Apgar** score. Most babies score 7 or above out of 10. A score of less than 7 indicates that help is needed.

	Scores 2	Scores 1	Scores 0
Pulse / Heartbeat	100 beats per minute	Less than 100 beats per minute	No pulse
Breathing	Regular	Irregular	None
Movements	Active	Some	Limp
Skin Colour	Pink	Bluish extremities	Totally blue
Reflexes	Crying	Whimpering	Silent

The Post-natal Period

Checks After Birth

Checks on babies after birth include facial features and body proportions, limbs and spine, hands (the number of creases on the palm could indicate Down's syndrome), umbilical cord, temperature, weight, length and head circumference.

Within 24 hours of birth a check is made for the passing of **meconium**: a black, sticky, tar-like bowel movement.

Further checks are made on ears (screening test for hearing), the fontanelles, the abdomen, the genitals, the hip joints (for congenital dislocation), the eyes and nose, and the nerves and muscles.

At 7–10 days, the **newborn blood spot screening** (NBSS) is done. It tests for **cystic fibrosis, sickle-cell anaemia** and **thalassaemia, PKU (phenyl-ketonuria)** and **thyroid function**. If the baby has PKU, a special diet is needed to prevent brain damage. For thyroid function, if the hormone thyroxin is lacking, treatment prevents abnormal growth and development.

About six weeks after birth, the mother has a post-natal appointment to check her emotional state, that her uterus has shrunk back to size and is tucked back into the pelvis, that any stitches have dissolved / wounds have healed, that her blood pressure is normal, and for post-natal bleeding.

Post-natal Depression

Hormonal changes, lack of sleep, and recovering from labour can cause mothers to feel miserable for a short time in the days after giving birth. This is called the **baby blues**, and **passes quickly**.

The baby blues shouldn't be confused with **post-natal depression**, where the mother feels overwhelmed and unable to cope. This illness can be treated with medication, counselling or support, but very occasionally requires psychiatric hospitalisation.

The Father's Role

After the birth, the baby's father should give the mother **emotional support**, e.g. listening to her, cuddling her, and being understanding. He should also provide **physical support**, e.g. with child care, housework, etc. Sometimes fathers feel left out,

especially if the baby is breastfed. Fathers need support too.

Fathers are entitled to two weeks' **paternity leave**, which must be taken within 8 weeks of the baby's birth. Fathers receive statutory paternity pay (SPP).

Quick Test

1. When does the umbilical cord drop off?
2. What is the average weight of a full-term baby?
3. What is another name for the Moro reflex?
4. What score do most babies have on an Apgar test?
5. Post-natal depression and baby blues are the same thing. **True** or **false**?

KEY WORDS
Make sure you understand these words before moving on!
- Fontanelles
- Reflex actions
- Meconium
- Newborn blood spot screening

Practice Questions

1 What is the Domino Delivery Scheme?

_____

_____

_____

2 Choose the correct words from the options given to complete the following sentences about pain relief in labour. Some words may be used more than once.

entonox	pethidine	TENS

epidural anaesthetic	water birth

a) _____ is inhaled through a mouthpiece or mask.

b) _____ uses electrical impulses to block pain.

c) An _____ _____ numbs the mother from the waist downwards.

d) A _____ _____ takes place in a birthing pool.

e) _____ is injected into a muscle.

f) An _____ _____ must be administered by an anaesthetist.

g) _____ is a mixture of nitrous oxide and oxygen.

h) _____ may cause a baby to be born drowsy.

3 What is labour?

_____

4 Choose the correct words from the options given to complete the following sentences.

irregular	1 minute	uterus	relaxes

Contractions start at _____ intervals. The _____ becomes tight for

up to _____ and then _____.

5 Fill in the missing words to complete the following table.

Birth Position	Description
a)	Baby lies across the uterus
b)	Baby lies at an angle in the uterus
c)	Baby has legs or bottom first

6 Which of the following are found in a SCBU? Tick the correct options.

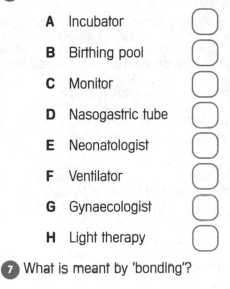

A   Incubator

B   Birthing pool

C   Monitor

D   Nasogastric tube

E   Neonatologist

F   Ventilator

G   Gynaecologist

H   Light therapy

7 What is meant by 'bonding'?

....

8 Which of the following isn't a reflex action present at birth? Tick the correct option.

A   Rooting

B   Holding

C   Falling

D   Sucking / swallowing

Nutrition

Macro Nutrient	Function	Source
Protein	Cell growth and repair	Meat, milk, fish, cheese, eggs, pulses, vegetables, nuts, soya, Quorn
Fat	Warmth and energy, protects internal organs	Butter, cream, cheese, oily fish, meat, nuts, oils, soya beans
Carbohydrates: sugar and starch	Provide energy	**Sugar**: honey, fruit, refined sugar **Starch**: flour, potatoes, pasta, rice, beans

Fibre / NSP aids digestion and prevents constipation. It's found in cereals, fruit and vegetables.

Micro Nutrient	Function	Source
Vitamin A	Healthy eyes and skin	Butter, margarine, carrots, green vegetables
Vitamin B group (includes folic acid)	Releases energy from food	Wholegrain cereals, meat, pulses
Vitamin C	Helps absorption of calcium and iron, protects against infections, heals wounds	Citrus fruits, strawberries, green vegetables, tomatoes
Vitamin D	Helps calcium absorption	Margarine, eggs, produced by action of sunlight on skin
Calcium	Strong bones and teeth	Milk, cheese, green vegetables
Iron	Carries oxygen in blood	Red meat, cocoa, green vegetables, dried fruit
Fluoride	Protects teeth	Seafood, fluoridated water

The **eatwell plate** has been provided as a guide for healthy eating by the Government's Food Standards Agency (FSA).

The different food groups are...

1. meat, fish, eggs, beans – eat some
2. fruit and vegetables – eat plenty
3. bread, rice, potatoes, pasta and other starchy foods – eat plenty
4. milk and dairy – eat some
5. foods and drinks high in fat and / or sugar – eat only in small amounts.

The eatwell plate isn't suitable for children under the age of two.

The eatwell plate

Use the eatwell plate to help you get the balance right. It shows how much of what you eat should come from each food group.

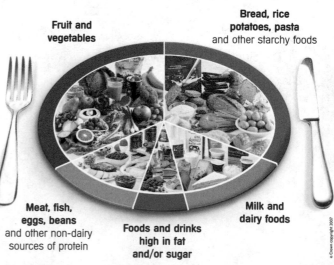

Fruit and vegetables

Bread, rice potatoes, pasta and other starchy foods

Meat, fish, eggs, beans and other non-dairy sources of protein

Foods and drinks high in fat and/or sugar

Milk and dairy foods

Obesity

Eating more food (calories) than the body needs for energy will result in **obesity**, because **excess calories** are **stored as fat**. Foods high in calories, e.g. fast food and confectionery, are specifically designed with children under 5/6 as the target market. The Government has introduced legislation to control advertising these foods. Parents need to disregard 'pester power' when shopping, because foods are packaged to attract children, e.g. using favourite characters. 'Junk' food, which may have a high fat/salt/sugar content but contains few nutrients, should be avoided. Foods high in sugar not only contribute to obesity, but also damage teeth.

Obesity can be caused by 'comfort eating' or through medical conditions, e.g. hormonal disorders.

Obesity Problems

A lifestyle that includes **physical activity** is essential for the health of children.

Children who are obese are more at risk of…
- coronary heart disease (CHD)
- high blood pressure
- type 2 diabetes
- problems with joints and bones
- infections
- becoming breathless in physical activities.

Obese children may be bullied or teased by peers, or have no friends. They may be self-conscious and have low self-esteem, and be embarrassed during physical activities.

Food Allergies and Intolerance

Children can be **intolerant** (e.g. to eggs) or allergic (e.g. to nuts) to **foods** and **chemical additives**.

An intolerance may be outgrown. An allergy is more serious and in severe cases can result in death. Foods that cause problems include eggs, wheat (coeliac), strawberries, nuts, dairy products (lactose intolerance) and shellfish. These foods should be avoided or replaced with alternative foods, e.g. soya milk. **Hyperactivity** has been linked with **tartrazine intolerance**.

Quick Test

1. Which nutrient is needed for growth and repair?
2. Who has provided the eatwell plate guidelines?
3. Foods are packaged to attract children.
   True or **false**?
4. Which is more serious – an intolerance or an allergy?

KEY WORDS
Make sure you understand these words before moving on!
- Macro nutrient
- Micro nutrient
- Eatwell plate
- Obesity
- Hyperactivity

Breastfeeding

Breastfeeding

Breastfeeding is a **natural process** controlled by prolactin. In the first days after birth **colostrum** is produced. This is a clear liquid that becomes yellow, containing protein and antibodies. When lactation (milk production) begins, a thin, bluish milk, which turns creamy at the end of a feed, is produced. Milk is squeezed out by the baby sucking the areola. The more a baby feeds, the more milk is produced.

Help with breastfeeding is available from midwives, health visitors and support groups, e.g. National Childbirth Trust (NCT) and La Leche League. The Government recommends breastfeeding exclusively for six months. Breast milk can be **expressed** and given in a bottle. It can be frozen and should be stored in sterile containers in the fridge if not for immediate use.

Mothers are **advised not to breastfeed** if they…
- are HIV positive or have AIDS
- are taking non-prescribed drugs or are dependent on them
- are taking cancer drugs or undergoing radiation treatment.

Mothers may also be advised not to breastfeed if they have had breast surgery or breast cancer.

Manual Breast Pump

Advantages for Mum and Baby

Breastfeeding has a number of **advantages** for the **mother**. Breastfeeding…
- is free and convenient
- helps bonding
- means that there's no preparation or sterilisation
- helps the mother to regain her figure faster
- helps the mother's uterus return to its previous size.

The **advantages** of breast milk for the **baby** are that it…
- contains the correct balance of nutrients, which automatically adjusts to the baby's needs
- contains antibodies
- contains polyunsaturated fatty acids for brain development
- is easy to digest
- doesn't contain additives.

There is also less likelihood of constipation, eczema, allergies and obesity for the baby.

Potential Problems

There are also potential problems with breastfeeding:
- embarrassment
- it can be tiring
- not enough milk is produced
- it can be difficult to return to work and go out
- sore, inverted nipples.

Bottle Feeding

Bottle Feeding

Mothers who choose not to breastfeed can bottle feed their babies with **formula milk** (modified cows' milk). Formula milk contains all the vitamins and minerals a baby needs, but doesn't offer the same degree of protection from infection as breastfeeding.

Some babies are allergic to cows' milk, and a soya-based formula may be used. Milk can be bought in powdered form to be reconstituted with water.

Different milks are produced for different ages. Liquid milk is useful for travelling or emergency use, but can be expensive and wasteful.

Sterilisation

There is a greater risk of babies developing illnesses and infections if bottles aren't made up correctly and hygienically.

All equipment must be carefully sterilised, as milk is a breeding ground for bacteria.

The two main methods of **sterilisation** are…

* **steam sterilisation**
* **cold water / chemical sterilisation**.

In an emergency bottles and teats can also be sterilised by boiling them for ten minutes.

Bottle Feeding Safely

When you're bottle feeding, you need **six bottles and teats**, a **bottle brush** and **sterilising equipment**.

Bottles should be an **easy shape to hold**, with a **wide neck**, the **correct size teats**, **graduated, easy to read measurements on the side**, and **able to be sealed for storage and travelling**.

Always…
* wash your hands thoroughly
* wash, rinse and sterilise all equipment
* make up feeds using the correct amount of freshly cooled boiled water and powder, following the manufacturer's instructions

* check the milk is the correct temperature before feeding
* make a fresh feed each time, and throw the feed away after an hour.

Never…
* make feeds too strong (this can lead to constipation, excess weight gain and other serious health conditions)
* microwave a feed, as dangerous 'hot spots' can occur
* reheat a feed
* use damaged equipment.

Quick Test

1. Colostrum is a clear liquid that turns yellow. **True** or **false**?
2. Can breast milk be expressed?
3. What kind of milk is used in bottle feeding?
4. What kind of water should you use to make up a bottle of formula milk?

KEY WORDS
Make sure you understand these words before moving on!
* Colostrum
* Expressed
* Formula milk
* Sterilisation

Weaning

Weaning

Weaning is mixed feeding. It's the gradual introduction of food to babies, and the reduction of milk consumption.

There are **three stages** of **weaning**.

The Department of Health recommends starting weaning at six months. After six months milk alone can't provide the correct amount of iron and other nutrients needed for growth and development. Weaning shouldn't be done before 17 weeks.

Any problems can be discussed with the health visitor.

Getting Started

Babies are ready to wean when they...
- still seem hungry after milk feeds
- start to wake up again in the night to be fed
- demand milk more often.

Weaning too early can cause...
- digestive problems
- allergies
- excess weight and food refusal in the future
- damage to kidneys.

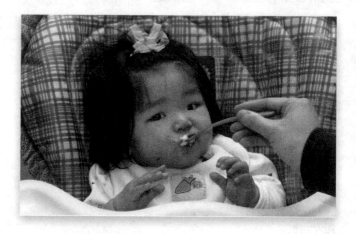

Stage 1 (6–7 months)

In **Stage 1** of weaning...
- offer food once a day in small amounts after a little milk
- purée food using a blender, or mash food with a fork to remove lumps, as the lumps can't be swallowed, chewed or digested
- don't give babies foods containing gluten
- introduce a variety of tastes
- encourage babies with smiles and talking
- serve the food at the same temperature as milk
- use sterile equipment.

If babies refuse a food, try it again later, or mix it with a food you know that they like.

Single-grain Cereals
Rice, sago, maize, millet, cornmeal, baby rice

Fruit
Bananas, apples, peaches, pears, mangos

Vegetables
Potatoes, carrots, parsnips, yams, courgettes, sweet potatoes

Stage 2 (7–9 months)

Babies can chew even without teeth, so food in Stage 2 of the weaning process should be mashed less thoroughly, or minced so that it has lumps. The lumps should gradually be increased in size.

In **Stage 2** of weaning…

- introduce wheat-based cereals and dairy products
- offer some **finger foods** (foods that babies can eat on their own, with supervision, by holding them in their hands), e.g. sandwiches, toast, low-sugar rusks, pieces of apple, banana, carrot, celery, cubes of cheese, pitta bread, chapatti (hard foods promote healthy teeth)
- use a beaker to offer water to drink
- give babies a spoon so that they can try to feed themselves.

Examples of Suitable Foods for Stage 2 of Weaning

Fruit
Pineapple, kiwi fruit, oranges, plums, etc.

Protein
Meat, fish, eggs (hard-boiled), cheese, soya beans

Vegetables
Pulse vegetables, cucumber, carrots, celery, cauliflower, broccoli, etc.

Stage 3 (9–12 months)

By Stage 3 of weaning, babies can eat the same food as the family three times a day. Food should be mashed or chopped if it can't be eaten with fingers.

In **Stage 3**, give healthy snacks and drinks between meals, as babies have small stomachs and use a lot of energy. At this stage of the weaning process, because babies are often hungry, they're willing to try new flavours and textures.

As the amount of solid food increases, the amount of milk decreases until only a bedtime milk feed is necessary. After 12 months the milk feed is for comfort rather than nutrition. From 12 months, full fat milk can be given.

Quick Test

1. What is another word for 'mixed feeding'?
2. There are three stages in weaning. **True** or **false**?
3. At what age can babies eat the same food as the family?
4. Do babies have large stomachs?

KEY WORDS

Make sure you understand these words before moving on!

- Weaning
- Stage 1 of weaning
- Stage 2 of weaning
- Finger foods
- Stage 3 of weaning

Children and Food

Types of Food Used for Weaning

Some foods are commercially produced for weaning.

Commercially prepared food has its **advantages**:
- It's convenient for travelling / in an emergency.
- It's easy to use and store.
- It contains adequate levels of nutrients (shown on the label).
- It's the correct consistency for different stages of weaning.
- It's hygienically produced.
- It's quick to prepare.
- There are different types available.
- Many of the foods are organic, so ingredients don't contain chemicals, fungicides, pesticides or synthetic drugs.
- Some foods have nutrients added, or are additive free.

The **disadvantages** of **commercially prepared food** are that it's more expensive, it has a bland flavour, some nutrients are removed by processing, and the portion size is pre-determined.

Preparing **home made food** has a range of **advantages**:
- Ingredients are fresh and more varied, with no additives (colourings, flavourings, preservatives).
- It's less expensive.
- There is less possibility of fussy eating.
- Portion size can be controlled.
- Food can be frozen.

The **disadvantages** of **home made food** are the preparation time, and that you need equipment, e.g. a blender.

Food Refusal

Food refusal is common in babies and children from 9 months to 4 years.

Children refuse to eat food because they're…
- not hungry, don't like the food, or are put off by the amount of food on their plate
- seeking attention or not cooperating
- tired, unwell or teething
- distracted, or wanting to play with the food.

Developing Healthy Eating Habits

Developing healthy eating habits sets the pattern for future behaviour. To develop healthy eating habits…
- the family should all eat the same food at regular mealtimes
- encourage independent eating, giving children their own cutlery and crockery
- avoid confrontation. To avoid stress, don't bribe or coax, force or threaten
- remove unwanted food without comment
- don't use food to comfort or reward
- serve small portions
- eat healthy balanced meals
- serve a variety of foods that have been cooked healthily
- make food look attractive
- let children shop and help cook, and sometimes choose the menu.

Causes and Symptoms

Food poisoning is caused by harmful bacteria, such as…

- **salmonella**
- **E-coli**
- listeria monocytogenes
- bacillus cereus
- staphylococcus aureus.

The symptoms of food poisoning include vomiting, diarrhoea, stomach cramps, fever and headaches.

Some food poisoning bacteria can cause death in children, and, if you are pregnant, can damage the foetus or lead to miscarriage.

Preventing Food Poisoning

If food is prepared, cooked and stored correctly, food poisoning can be prevented.

1 Practise good personal hygiene:
- Don't lick fingers or bowls.
- Don't cough, sneeze or smoke over food.
- Don't touch spots or pick scabs.
- Keep nails short and clean.
- Wash hands thoroughly.

2 In the kitchen…
- clean all equipment, cutlery, etc. thoroughly with hot soapy water
- sterilise babies' feeding equipment
- clean work surfaces, sinks, etc. with antibacterial cleaner
- ensure that all foods, especially cook-chill meals, are correctly heated
- throw away any left-over reheated food
- empty the rubbish bin regularly
- keep pets out, and use separate cutlery and bowls for them.

3 Store food correctly:
- Use sell-by and use-by dates correctly.
- Keep food covered.
- Follow storage instructions on labels.
- Keep the fridge temperature between 1°C and 4°C, and the freezer at -18°C.
- Avoid **cross contamination** (transfer of bacteria) by keeping raw food and cooked food apart.

Quick Test

1. Commercially prepared food is cheaper than home made food. **True** or **false**?
2. To develop healthy eating habits, what should you do with unwanted food?
3. Can food poisoning lead to miscarriage?
4. For good personal hygiene, what should finger nails be like?

KEY WORDS
Make sure you understand these words before moving on!
- Food refusal
- Salmonella
- E-coli
- Cross contamination

Practice Questions

1. Which of the following is a micro nutrient? Tick the correct option.

   A   Non starch polysaccharide ⬭

   B   Calcium ⬭

   C   Protein ⬭

   D   Fat ⬭

2. Circle the correct options in the following sentences.

   a) **Vitamin A** / **Vitamin D** is needed for healthy eyes and skin.

   b) **Vitamin C** / **Vitamin B** is found in citrus fruits.

   c) **Calcium** / **iron** carries oxygen in the blood.

   d) **Iron** / **fluoride** protects teeth.

3. Choose the correct words from the options given to complete the following sentences.

legislation	advertising	confectionery	children
calories	Government	target market	

   a) Foods high in ...., e.g. fast food and ...., are specifically

   designed with .... under 5 / 6 as the ....

   ....

   b) The .... has introduced .... to

   control the .... of these foods.

4. Fill in the missing words to complete the following sentence.

   In the first few days after birth .... is produced. It is a ....

   liquid, which becomes ....

5 Which of the following statements is true? Tick the correct option.

A Milk is squeezed out by the baby sucking the nipple. ◯

B Breast milk can't be given in a bottle. ◯

C Formula milk contains antibodies. ◯

D Breast milk contains bacteria. ◯

E Formula milk is easier to digest than breast milk. ◯

F Some babies are allergic to breast milk. ◯

G Formula milk can be made from soya. ◯

H Formula milk doesn't contain vitamins. ◯

6 Fill in the missing words to complete the following sentence.

At Stage 2 of weaning, babies can _____ food, even without _____ ,

so their food should contain _____ .

7 Which of the following statements is correct? Tick the correct option.

A Home made food contains additives. ◯

B Home made food is bland. ◯

C Home made food is quick to prepare. ◯

D Home made food can be frozen. ◯

8 Circle the correct options in the following sentences.

a) Children may refuse to eat food if they're given **too much** / **too little** on their plate.

b) Children who **are hungry** / **aren't hungry** may refuse to eat.

c) Children may refuse to eat if they're **wet** / **teething**.

d) Children may refuse to eat food because they **do** / **don't** like it.

9 How can food poisoning be prevented?

_____

_____

Areas of Development

Areas of Development

There are four areas of development:

- **physical**
- **intellectual**
- **emotional**
- **social**.

These four areas are sometimes represented by the word **PIES**.

Development isn't the same as growth. Growth is an increase in size, weight and height. It's checked and recorded on **centile charts**.

PIES developments are closely interlinked. Children can't develop the social skills of feeding, dressing or washing themselves without the necessary physical skills. Toilet training, a social skill, isn't possible without physical control of the bladder and bowel. If children are emotionally insecure, their intellectual development will be delayed.

The same sequence and pattern of development is seen in most children, except some children who have a genetic disability, e.g. Down's syndrome, or a congenital disorder, e.g. cerebral palsy.

Milestones

Milestones are guidelines for when major achievements will happen, e.g. when children master a new skill such as walking.

A **milestone** is the stage that most children will have reached by a certain age. Milestones are only an indication, because all children develop at their own pace.

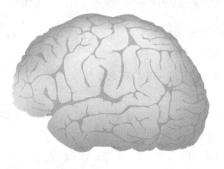

Intellectual Development

Intellectual development refers to the development of the mind / brain. It is the child's ability to learn, reason and understand language. Intellectual development includes reading, writing, drawing, number skills, imagination, creativity, hypothesis (predicting what might happen in the future), and understanding concepts.

Concepts

Understanding **concepts** takes a long time to develop. It starts with general ideas and understanding of physical things that can be seen or felt, e.g. colours and shapes. It then progresses to abstract things like morals, e.g. right and wrong.

Concepts include rhythm, space, time, volume, mass / weight, size, shape, living / non living, object permanence.

From birth babies try to make sense of what is happening around them when any of their senses are aroused. This is called **stimulation**.

Some people believe that children are born with their talents and abilities (intelligence) pre-determined by their genes (nature). Others believe that it's the effect of their environment (nurture) that's important. What is most likely is that both have an effect.

Intellectual Development

How Do Children Learn?

Children learn through exploration, play, repetition and practice, imitation (copying), experience and observation. They also learn by asking questions.

How To Help Intellectual Development

You can help intellectual development…
- through love, encouragement, support, praise and quality time
- by doing activities that teach rhymes, the alphabet, numbers, etc.
- through stimulation and providing suitable toys
- by having a healthy diet
- by visiting new places, reading books, watching educational television and DVDs
- by talking and listening, by answering questions and explaining information
- by providing a suitable environment.

The table shows examples of age-related activities that stimulate intellectual development.

Age	Activities
Newborn	Make a face for baby to copy; hold brightly coloured, shiny or contrasting black and white patterns near to the baby and move slowly; sing; allow freedom to kick without clothes on (not all babies like this)
3 months	Change baby's position and location to stimulate senses and prevent boredom
6 months	Action rhymes
9 months	Peek-a-boo and hide-and-seek type games
12 months	Games using hands, e.g. one potato, two potatoes; mother and toddler groups
18 months	Feely bag, i.e. a bag or box containing objects that the child can identify only by touch; action games and songs
2–3 years	Make musical instruments and play them; simple cooking and baking; games of make believe (imaginative play); visit the library and park, etc.; playgroup
3–4 years	Games such as musical statues; encourage responsibility for household tasks, e.g. setting the table
4–5 years	Visit museums, theatre, cinema

Quick Test

1. A milestone is a guideline. **True** or **false**?
2. Which area of development is linked with learning?
3. What is the name for predicting what might happen in the future?
4. What are time and volume examples of?

KEY WORDS

Make sure you understand these words before moving on!
- Milestone
- Intellectual development
- Concepts

Writing and Drawing

Writing and Drawing

To write and draw takes **practice** and **repetition**, so the pencil, crayon, etc. can be controlled.

Children need a range of materials and large sheets of paper to let them experiment. A drawing isn't always produced. Sometimes a picture is scribbled over because the experience is more important than the end result. Children are proud of their creations and like to see them displayed.

Through drawing, and later writing, children can express their ideas, thoughts and feelings, and use their imagination.

	Age (approx.)				
	15 months	**18 months**	**2–3 years**	**4 years**	**5–6 years**
Pencil and crayon control	**Palmar grasp** Crayon held half-way up	**Primitive tripod grasp** Using the thumb and first two fingers; may use preferred hand	**Tripod grasp** Good pencil control; uses preferred hand	Holds pencil well in correct way	Good control of pencil
Drawing	Scribbles to and fro, not lifting crayon from paper	Scribbles to and fro, but can lift crayon from paper to draw dots	Recognisable circle; can copy / draw T, V and H; draws a person with squiggle features, which becomes more detailed	Can copy OX; can trace over words; figures have head, body, legs and arms, fingers and toes	May write own name; adds clothes, hair and features to the body when drawing people; can draw house, etc.; pictures have background details; can colour inside lines
Examples					

Speech and Language Development

The pattern of speech development is…

1 pre-linguistic

2 linguistic.

From birth to 12 months, in the **pre-linguistic stage**, communication is by sounds. Babies communicate their needs by crying when they're thirsty, hungry, tired, lonely, uncomfortable, in pain, ill, or too hot / cold.

Age	Sounds
5 / 6 weeks	Gurgles and coos
6 months	**Babbles**; says 'aa', 'oo', 'ddd', 'mmm'; **echolalia**, i.e. repetitive sounds like dada, ma ma, and goo, der, ka, adah
9 months	Says mum-mum, bab-bab
1 year	**Holophrases**, i.e. expresses an idea in one word, e.g. mama, cat

The **linguistic stage** is from 12 months. Single words become simple, then complex sentences.

Age	Speech
18 months	Uses **6–40 identifiable words** with expression
2 years	**Telegraphic speech**, i.e. uses crucial words, e.g. where cat?, me want cake
$2\frac{1}{2}$–3 years	**200+ word vocabulary**; uses 'I', 'me', 'you' correctly; asks questions like Why?, What?, Who?; is understood outside the family; word endings are incorrect, e.g. I 'runned'
4–5 years	Talks fluently using complex sentences; a few mistakes in grammar and pronunciation; good articulation; **large vocabulary of 2000+ words**

Encouraging Speech

You can encourage speech by…

- constant verbal interaction from birth
- giving children time to speak, and not finishing their sentences for them
- not interrupting when a child is speaking
- not laughing at children's mistakes
- using 'open' questions that need more than a 'yes' or 'no' answer.

Quick Test

1 At what age would the palmar grasp be used on a crayon?
2 How do babies communicate?
3 At what age is echolalia used?
4 At what age is telegraphic speech used?

KEY WORDS

Make sure you understand these words before moving on!

- Pre-linguistic stage
- Echolalia
- Holophrases
- Linguistic stage

Physical Development

What is Physical Development?

Physical development can be…
- **sensory** development
- **motor** development.

Sensory development relates to sight, hearing, touch, taste and smell.

Motor development relates to the body.

There are two sets of skills involved in motor development:
- **Gross motor** / **major motor skills** are the use and control of large muscles, e.g. walking, kicking, running.
- **Fine motor** / **manipulative skills** are the control and use of hands and fingers, e.g. pincer grip, fastening buttons.

Milestones 0–1 year

Age	Physical Milestones
Newborn	Reflexes, e.g. Moro, walking; no head control; sees vague shapes, light movement
1 month	Tracks objects
3 months	Held upright, legs bear a little weight; more head control; needs help to sit; kicks vigorously using alternate legs; raises head and chest using forearms; hands open, can hold objects
6 months	Head fully controlled and can turn; holds one or both feet lying on back; legs bear weight when held upright; on front supports head and chest with straight arms; rolls from back to front; holds arms out to be picked up; reaches for objects using palmar grasp to pass hand to hand; eyes work together
9 months	Pulls into sitting and standing position; sits unsupported; deliberately drops objects; crawls on hands and knees / feet; shuffles on bottom; bear walks; rolls, wriggles to move; walks when both hands are held; can use finger and thumb to grasp an object (inferior pincer grip)
12 months	Walks with one hand held; 'cruises' with feet wide apart; uses primitive tripod grip; helps with dressing; deliberately throws objects; focuses on distant objects

Physical Development

Age	Physical Milestones
15 months	Walks independently, using arms to balance; walks upstairs forwards, downstairs backwards; kneels; builds a 2 brick tower; uses cup and spoon
18 months	Walks confidently; walks upstairs putting both feet on each step; controls wrist, e.g. turns knobs; removes shoes and socks; builds a 2–3 brick tower
2 years	Runs, avoiding obstacles; walks on tiptoe; jumps; kicks ball; uses preferred hand; threads beads; builds a 6–8 brick tower; starts potty training
3 years	Walks upstairs one foot on each step, downstairs with 2 feet; balances on 1 leg; walks sideways; pedals and steers toys; throws ball overarm and catches it; dresses and undresses with help
4 years	Goes up and down stairs like an adult; has a mature pincer grip; eats skilfully with a spoon and fork; uses a bat with a ball; improved balance and climbing skills
5 years	Dresses and undresses mostly independently; uses knife and fork well; increased agility; can skip, dance rhythmically and use large equipment confidently

Quick Test

1. Which muscles are controlled in gross motor development?
2. What is another name for fine motor skills?
3. By what age can a baby fully control its head?
4. At what age can a child run, avoiding obstacles?
5. By the age of 4 a child can use a knife and fork well. **True** or **false**?

KEY WORDS

Make sure you understand these words before moving on!
- Gross motor skills
- Fine motor skills

Emotional Development

Emotional Development

It takes time for children to learn how to recognise and control their feelings (emotions), so they can behave in a socially acceptable way. **Emotions** can be **positive** or **negative**.

Positive Emotions		Negative Emotions		
☺ Excitement ☺ Happiness		☹ Anger	☹ Frustration	☹ Guilt
☺ Pleasure ☺ Joy		☹ Aggression	☹ Jealousy	☹ Fear
☺ Pride ☺ Contentment		☹ Shyness	☹ Hate	☹ Distress
☺ Affection ☺ Love		☹ Sadness	☹ Rudeness	☹ Disgust

Stages of Emotional Development

These are the stages of emotional development:
- **Newborn** – uses body to express emotion
- **3 months** – smiles and coos to show pleasure
- **6 months** – separation anxiety begins, the child is distressed if the main carer isn't there; laughs and enjoys being played with
- **9 months** – expresses anger; afraid of strangers; may use a comfort object like a dummy, toy blanket or thumb, which soothes them at once

Comforter	Advantage	Disadvantage
Dummy	Parent can control use; easy to replace	Needs sterilising; can affect teeth and speech
Thumb	Child controls it; always available	Sore thumb; difficult habit to break
Blanket / toy	Causes no physical harm	Gets lost, dirty

- **12 months** – seeks attention and reassurance from known adults; affectionate; shy with strangers
- **15 months** – rapid mood swings
- **18 months** – expresses frustration, rage, fear, happiness
- **2 years** – very **egocentric**, believing that the whole world should revolve around them. They want things **now**. This lack of emotional control and frustration can result in **temper tantrums**. This stage is called the **terrible twos**, but can happen at other ages
- **3 years** – cares for others and can empathise; may develop fears, e.g. of the dark
- **4 years** – affectionate; strong-willed; sense of humour
- **5 years** – happy to leave parents for longer; enjoys caring for pets.

Temper Tantrums

Temper tantrums are more common when a child is over tired, attention seeking, jealous, reacting to colourings and E numbers, bored, not wanting to share, or unhappy.

To deal with tantrums you should…
- keep calm, be patient, and don't shout or smack
- explain that it's not acceptable behaviour
- be consistent and don't reward bad behaviour
- ignore or distract, and be a good role model
- avoid situations leading to tantrums
- use a 'naughty step'
- cuddle the child afterwards.

Helping Emotional Development

There are a number of ways to help emotional development:

1. Encourage children to express their feelings, e.g. through role play, drawing, play dough, soft toys, hammering on a drum.
2. Develop independence by…
   - giving children choices
   - avoiding power struggles
   - accepting that defiance and disobedience are an integral part of becoming independent
   - having reasonable expectations.
3. Provide secure relationships / bonding and good role models.
4. Encourage socialisation, talking and communication.

5. Build **self-esteem**, so that children feel confident about themselves. Do this by…
   - praising rather than criticising
   - not laughing at children
   - accepting children as individuals, avoiding comparing them with others
   - providing suitable, fair and consistent discipline.

Negative Feelings

Factors that negatively affect emotional development include the death of a pet / person, boredom, frustration, change of routine, starting playgroup / nursery / school, change of carer, new baby, moving house, illness, abuse, neglect, and inadequate or excessive discipline.

These feelings may be expressed as **insecurity** and cause **separation anxiety** or nightmares. Bad behaviour results.

There may be **sibling rivalry** when older brothers and sisters (siblings) feel jealous when a new baby arrives.

Resenting the attention given to the baby, they may become clingy, withdrawn, uncooperative, aggressive (e.g. biting, nipping, pinching), or regress in behaviour.

Regression takes place when a child regresses (goes back) temporarily to an earlier stage of development, e.g. demands to be fed.

Quick Test

1. In what two ways can emotions be expressed?
2. At what age does a baby have rapid mood swings?
3. At what age do temper tantrums start?
4. Negative feelings make a child feel good. **True** or **false**?

KEY WORDS

Make sure you understand these words before moving on!
- Egocentric
- Self-esteem
- Insecurity
- Separation anxiety
- Sibling rivalry
- Regression

Social Development

Social Skills

Socialisation lets children fit in with the people who live with and around them.

Socialisation is the acquisition of skills such as...
- being able to respect the ideas and feelings of others
- making friends
- sharing and taking turns
- cooperating and negotiating
- understanding rules
- eating correctly
- having standards of hygiene.

Social Experiences

Social experiences should be appropriate to the child's age, and provide the opportunity to mix and communicate with other people.

Examples are parties, holidays, visiting relatives and friends, visiting church and Sunday school, the park, zoo, museum, farm, ball pool, going to nursery / playgroup, and dance, drama, music and swimming lessons.

Stages of Social Development

These are the stages of social development:
- **First weeks** – responds to main carer with smiles and gurgles
- **3 months** – has 'conversations' by making noise; enjoys others' company
- **6 months** – attracts adult attention to start interaction; shy with strangers; reacts differently to cross and pleasant voices; uses fingers to feed themselves
- **12 months** – understands basic commands, e.g. waves bye bye; helps with daily routine, e.g. lifts legs for nappy change; drinks from cup and uses spoon
- **2 years** – self feeds; starts toilet training; parallel play
- **3 years** – uses toilet mostly independently; willing to share and take turns; likes to be with other children, chooses own friends
- **4–5 years** – shares well and understands rules; less demanding of adult attention.

Social Development

Encouraging Social Skills

Encourage **social skills** by…
- reinforcing acceptable behaviour in a loving, secure environment
- encouraging independence
- building self-esteem.

Negative / Anti-social Behaviour

If children behave in a **negative** and **anti-social** way, this can result in **social isolation** (having no friends).

Examples of these behaviours include…
- lying
- **aggression**, e.g. kicking, biting, punching, shouting
- temper tantrums
- teasing and bullying; spoiling games and damaging others' work
- seeking attention, e.g. refusing to eat / use the toilet, screaming, holding breath, refusing to cooperate
- self-harm, e.g. head banging.

Discipline

Discipline helps a child to behave in an acceptable way, and leads to self-discipline. Discipline should be appropriate for a child's age, ability and understanding.

Be firm, fair and consistent, with no idle threats. Set clear boundaries and don't have too many rules. Don't use physical punishment. Show disapproval by…
- not giving eye contact
- not speaking to the child, or using a stern voice
- looking disinterested
- lack of body contact (unless safety is an issue).

Praise, encourage and reward good behaviour. Show approval by…
- smiling
- touching
- playing with the child
- using reward charts.

Deal with problems immediately, and explain to the child what the problems are. Give the child a warning before you punish them. Punishment could be taking away an activity or toy, or spending time in a 'naughty spot' or 'naughty chair'.

Quick Test

1. Making friends is a social skill. **True** or **false**?
2. At what age is a baby shy with strangers?
3. At what age do children share and take turns?
4. You should show disapproval by physical punishment. **True** or **false**?

KEY WORDS

Make sure you understand these words before moving on!
- Social skills
- Negative / Anti-social
- Aggression
- Discipline

Toys, Books and Television

Toys

When you're **choosing toys**, check that they…
- are suitable for age and ability
- have a safety CE mark / Kitemark / **Lion Mark**
- are strong / stable / have no sharp edges
- are non-toxic and lead free
- are non-flammable or flame resistant
- are washable (for babies).

Regular checks should be made for damage and loose parts, and you should make sure that batteries for toys aren't accessible to children.

Computerised toys can help with number / letter / colour recognition. Many computerised toys make sounds.

ages 3-8 years
sizzlin' kitchen accessory set

Age	Suggested Toys – Examples
0–6 months	Rattles; mobiles; soft toys; musical toys; bath toys; baby mirror; bouncing cradle; activity mat
6–12 months	Stacking beakers; push and pull toys; building bricks
12–18 months	Pop-up toys; sand; shape sorters; rocking toys; sit-and-ride toys; push and pull toys
18 months–2 years	Simple large-piece jigsaws; balls; Duplo; toys with moving parts; small swing; slide; paddling pool
2–3 years	Pencils; crayons; play dough; more complex jigsaws; threading beads; fuzzy felt; picture dominoes; simple climbing frame; dressing-up clothes; tricycle; car; small pram; dolls
3–4 years	Bike; dressing-up clothes; construction toys; simple board games; picture dominoes
4–5 years	As above, plus counting games; clock; baking utensils; gardening equipment; skipping rope; rollerskates; materials for creative work

Books and Television

Considerations when choosing books should include…
- the child's age and interests
- the size of the print and pages
- the number of pages
- the material, e.g. card / paper / plastic / fabric
- content – everyday objects for 0–1 year olds; detailed stories about everyday events or fictional characters for 3–5 year olds
- special features, e.g. pop-up, noise, lift the flap, texture, smell
- illustrations – simple and colourful for 0–1 year olds; detailed for 3–5 year olds.

Bookstart provides **free** packs at 7–9 months, approx. 18–30 months, and for 3–4 year olds.

Encourage reading by having lots of books within easy reach, visiting a library, letting your child choose books, making reading fun, and being a good role model who reads yourself. Don't just read at bedtime. Have special times in the day when you read and have cuddles.

Television, **DVDs** and **videos** should have a good educational context, be watched for a limited time, **with** an adult, and talked about afterwards. Television shouldn't be used as a babysitter.

Play / Stages of Play

Play lets children make sense of the world, and develop physically, intellectually, emotionally and socially (PIES). Children play instinctively. **Structured play** is organised by others. **Spontaneous play** happens on the spur of the moment, is initiated (started) by the child, and there's no adult interference.

Children who are denied access to a range of stimulating play activities have **play malnourishment**. Possible consequences of being play malnourished are poor neurological development, more violent, anti-social, aggressive behaviour, and being unfit and obese.

The stages of play development are…

- **solitary play** (0–2 years) – children play alone, e.g. baby with a rattle, toddler with a puzzle
- **parallel play** (2 years) – children play alongside, but not with each other (no interaction)
- **looking on play** (3 years) – children just watch others, but don't join in
- **joining-in play** (3 years) – children do the same activity, but in their own way
- **cooperative play** (3+ years) – children play together.

Types of Play

There are different types of play:

- In **creative play**, children use their imaginations, e.g. dancing, making music. It can be messy, e.g. cutting and sticking.
- **Imaginative play** is also called pretend, role, fantasy and superhero play. Children pretend to be characters and make up games and scenarios.
- In **physical play** the body is used in an active way, so space is needed. It often takes place outdoors, e.g. riding a bike, but may be indoors, e.g. in the home, or at a ball pool or swimming pool.

- **Manipulative play** develops hand-eye coordination and fine motor skills, e.g. playing with a rattle, jigsaw, building with Duplo or bricks, and sand and water play.
- **Discovery** (exploratory, intellectual) **play** uses the senses, e.g. babies 'mouth' objects to find out about them. Sand / water play lets scientific concepts be investigated.
- **Social play** helps children learn to cooperate, share and take turns, understand rules, and make friends.

Quick Test

1. Children aged 0–1 years need detailed pictures in books. **True** or **false**?
2. Name the stage of play where children play alone.
3. What type of play is it when children play together?
4. What kind of play usually takes place outdoors?

KEY WORDS

Make sure you understand these words before moving on!
- Lion Mark
- Solitary play
- Parallel play
- Looking on play
- Joining in play
- Cooperative play

Practice Questions

1 Which of the following isn't a concept? Tick the correct option.

    A Time ◯

    B Play ◯

    C Shape ◯

    D Rhythm ◯

2 Fill in the missing word to complete the following sentence.

_____ development is the development of the brain.

3 Circle the correct options in the following sentences.

    a) At 5–6 weeks a baby **gurgles** / **babbles**.

    b) At 6 months a baby can say **cat** / **adah**.

    c) At 2 years, a child uses **holophrases** / **telegraphic speech**.

    d) A 4–5 year old child has a vocabulary of **200+** / **2000+** words.

4 Choose the correct ages from the options given to complete the following sentences.

    2 year   **15 month**   **12 month**   **9 month**

A _____ old tiptoes. A _____ old 'cruises'. A _____ old uses their arms to balance when walking. A _____ old sits unaided.

5 Which of the following isn't a comfort object? Tick the correct option.

    A Dummy ◯

    B Disposable nappy ◯

    C Blanket ◯

    D Thumb ◯

6 Fill in the missing words to complete the following sentence.

_____ play is also called _____ play, _____ play, fantasy play and _____ play.

7 Which of the following are social skills? Tick the correct options.

A Drawing ⬭

B Eating correctly ⬭

C Baking ⬭

D Making friends ⬭

E Cooperating ⬭

F Reading ⬭

G Sharing ⬭

H Swimming ⬭

8 Choose the correct words from the options given to complete the following sentences.

stacking   **sit-and-ride horse**   **mobile**   **skipping rope**

A .... is a suitable toy for a 4–5 year old. A

.... is a suitable toy for a 12–18 month old child.

A .... is suitable for a 0–6 month old baby. A .... toy is

suitable for a 6–12 month old baby.

9 Choose the correct words from the options given to complete the following sentences.

manipulative   **role**   **creative**   **social**

exploratory   **physical**

a) .... play helps children to understand rules.

b) .... play uses the body in an active way.

c) .... play is also known as discovery play.

d) .... play helps develop hand-eye coordination.

e) .... play is also known as imaginative play.

f) .... play uses the imagination.

Health and Safety

First Aid Box

A **first aid box** should be **accessible**, and **used items** should be **replaced** quickly. Items that have reached their expiry date should also be replaced.

Contents include plasters, an eye bath, scissors, calamine lotion, bandages, tweezers, and antiseptic wipes / cream.

Over the counter medicines like Calpol and prescribed drugs must be kept out of the reach of children, and stored and used according to the instructions given.

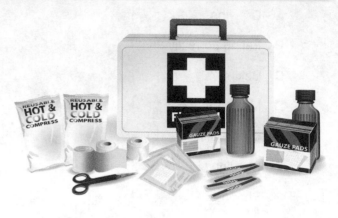

Accidents and Injuries

Always stay calm when there has been an accident, and comfort and reassure the child.

Problem	What to Do
Cuts, grazes, scratches	Clean with cool boiled water / antiseptic wipe, leave uncovered, use plaster if necessary
Deep wound	Apply pressure; stitches may be needed
Bruise	Cold compress
Nose bleed	Firmly pinch the bridge of the nose for 10 minutes, sit child upright, slightly forward, repeat up to 3 times; if bleeding continues, seek medical help
Choking	Lay baby across forearm with head forward, pat back 4 / 5 times; put an older child downwards over your knee and slap 4 / 5 times between shoulder blades; if this doesn't work hold the child's waist, ask them to cough, and pull up sharply below ribs
Electric shock	Switch off power or push child away from electric source with non-metallic object, check for pulse, resuscitate if necessary
Object in eye	Remove object(s) from corner of the eye with clean cloth, from eye ball with eye bath; wash out chemicals immediately
Stings (insects / plants)	Remove insect sting with tweezers if appropriate; use calamine lotion or anti-histamine cream
Burns (dry heat)	For small burns place affected part in cold water for 10 minutes, pat dry, cover with gauze dressing; don't use plasters, creams, or prick the blisters
Scalds (moist heat)	For large severe burns as above, but if burn is larger than a child's hand, severely blistered or has broken the skin, take child to hospital immediately
Broken bones	Keep injured part immobile; seek medical help
Poison	Don't make the child sick; take the child to hospital with a sample of the poison

Parasites

Facts About Parasites

A **parasite** is an organism that lives on another organism, obtaining food from it. Parasites are easily 'caught' but are also easy to treat. Except for roundworms, they are harmless, but socially unacceptable. You should deal with them quickly so they don't multiply.

Parasite	Signs and Symptoms	How Spread	Prevention and Treatment
Headlice	Itchy red bite marks on scalp; grey / brown nits (eggs) attached to hair; white / shiny empty egg cases on hair	Head-to-head contact	Leave conditioner on hair and wet-comb with detector (nit) comb; use chemical shampoo treatment; use 'electric' comb
Scabies	Irritating skin rash; mite 'burrows' are seen; if scratched rash produces septic spots	Direct skin-to-skin contact	Treat **all** family with lotion from GP; thoroughly wash towels, bed linen and clothing
Fleas	Small red bite marks	Jump long distances onto other people	Ensure people, houses and clothes are clean; treat pets for fleas
Threadworms	Itching around anus; worms visible in faeces or around anus	Swallowing eggs	Strict hygiene, e.g. thorough hand washing; bath or shower each morning; medicate **whole** family
Roundworms	Fever; vomiting; painful muscles and joints; damage to eyesight	Swallowing eggs from animal faeces	Strict pet hygiene – wash hands after playing with pets; safe disposal of animal faeces; regular pet 'worming'; medicate **whole** family

Quick Test

1. You should place burns in cold water for 10 minutes. **True** or **false**?
2. How are headlice spread?
3. Parasites are difficult to treat. **True** or **false**?
4. Which parasite is visible in faeces?

KEY WORDS

Make sure you understand these words before moving on!
- Parasite
- Headlice
- Scabies
- Fleas
- Threadworms
- Roundworms

Childhood Illnesses

Signs of Illness

Most children get ill at some time, and can be treated at home.

Signs of illness include…

- a raised or lowered temperature
- perspiration
- vomiting or nausea
- diarrhoea or constipation
- swollen glands
- joint pain
- a cough, headache, stomach ache, runny nose or earache
- pale / flushed skin or rash
- difficulty breathing
- changed behaviour, e.g. crying more than usual or a changed sleep pattern.

Ear Thermometer

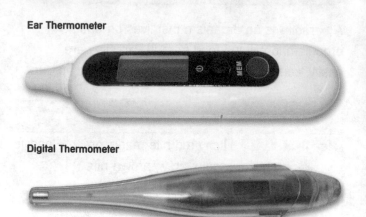

Digital Thermometer

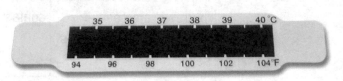

Forehead Thermometer

| 35 | 36 | 37 | 38 | 39 | 40 °C |
| 94 | 96 | 98 | 100 | 102 | 104 °F |

Illnesses

Illness	How to Recognise	What to Do	Infectious Period
Mumps	Slight fever; earache; swollen gland in front of ear(s)	Paracetamol; drinks (not fruit juice)	Few days before symptoms show until swelling goes down
Chicken pox	Rash; small red patches develop into blisters, which turn crusty and fall off	Paracetamol; baths; loose clothing; calamine lotion	Day before rash until spots are dry
Measles	Cough / cold; sore watery eyes; red blotchy rash	Paracetamol; drinks	Few days before until 4 days after rash
Rubella (German measles)	Mild cold; pink rash; pink spots that merge together	Drinks	One week before to 4 days after rash
Whooping cough (Pertussis)	Cold / cough that develops into exhausting coughing bouts, making breathing difficult	Seek medical help for antibiotic treatment	5 days after antibiotic treatment starts; up to 6 weeks without antibiotic treatment
Tuberculosis	Cough; fever (can mimic other diseases)	Seek medical help for antibiotic treatment	Up to 6 weeks after inhaling bacteria
Meningitis	Headache; fever; stiff neck; aching joints; dislike of light; severe sleepiness; fine red / purple rash that doesn't fade under pressure	Seek urgent medical help	1–2 weeks before symptoms until several weeks after

Caring for a Sick Child

When children are unwell…
- comfort and cuddle them
- give them your time and attention
- give them appropriate medicine, following the storage and dosage instructions
- encourage visitors
- give them lots of drinks
- provide varied activities and entertainment
- check their temperature.

Taking and Reducing Temperature

A **normal temperature** is **37°C**. It can be checked quickly and accurately using an ear or digital **thermometer**. These thermometers are safe to use and give clear, easy to read, figures. A forehead thermometer has liquid crystals that change colour. It's less accurate.

Reducing a high temperature decreases the risk of convulsions (fits).

Reduce your child's high temperature by…
- sponging or bathing them in lukewarm water
- removing clothing (except nappy)
- using a fan to maintain room temperature at 15°C
- removing blankets / duvets from bed
- giving them the correct dose of paracetamol.

When to Seek Help

Get help from your GP or **NHS Direct** if your child has a temperature over 39°C, a severe cough, persistent earache / headache, or hasn't passed urine in the last 12 hours.

Get help from hospital if your child has…
- a sunken fontanelle
- breathing difficulties
- bloody stools
- constant diarrhoea
- become unconscious, or abnormally floppy
- refused liquid for 12 hours
- swallowed a dangerous object, e.g. battery, medicine, bleach
- a purple / red rash that doesn't fade with pressure.

You should also get help from hospital if your child is coughing up blood.

Quick Test

1. Which illness gives a child swollen glands in front of the ear(s)?
2. What is another name for whooping cough?
3. Sick children don't need to be given activities and entertainment. **True** or **false**?
4. What risk decreases if a high temperature is lowered?

KEY WORDS
Make sure you understand these words before moving on!
- Temperature
- Thermometer
- NHS Direct

Staying in Hospital

Staying in Hospital

A hospital stay can be difficult, traumatic and upsetting because of...

- strange surroundings and unfamiliar people
- a different routine
- absent family members
- unpleasant, uncomfortable treatment or pain.

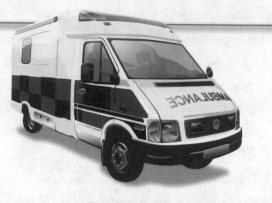

Making it a Happier Experience

A hospital stay can be made easier for children when there's unrestricted visiting and parents can stay overnight.

A **pre-admission visit** for a **non-emergency**, e.g. a minor operation, will reassure children. They're shown equipment and encouraged to play with it.

Parents should let children pack their own bags, remembering a comfort toy. Let them choose something new to take with them, e.g. pyjamas.

Parents can explain about hospitals as a precaution in case of **emergency admission**, e.g. for an asthma attack. Depending on the child's age, they can...

- use books, DVDs, stories, games
- explain what might happen, with emphasis on being made well
- encourage role play by providing nurses' and doctors' outfits, and 'pretend' medical equipment.

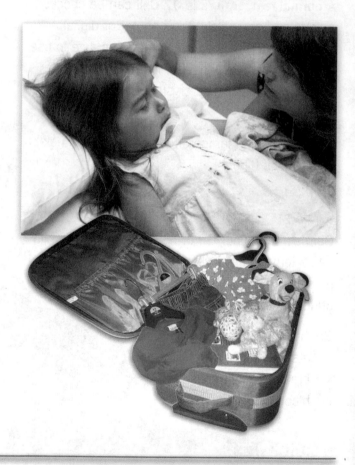

Regression

Any illness can affect developmental progress in a negative way, resulting in regression. **Regression** is when children temporarily return to **behaviour** they showed when they were **younger**, e.g. bed wetting, temper tantrums, demanding help with feeding.

Patience, understanding, and lots of love and attention solve this problem.

The Importance of Immunisation

The immunisation programme begins at 2 months, and is a way of **protecting** babies against serious diseases. The **vaccines** make babies' bodies develop their own **defence system** by producing **antibodies**. Once immunised, a body is able to recognise certain infections and diseases, and fight them off. Some of these diseases can be life threatening.

It's very important that babies are immunised at the right age. Most children can be immunised safely.

A child's health is at greater risk from the diseases than the vaccines. There may be some side effects after immunisation, such as swelling at the site of the injection, a mild rash, or raised temperature.

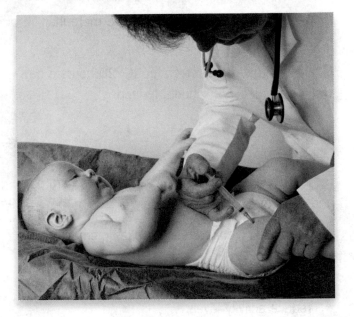

Immunisation Programme

Each vaccine or group of vaccines represents a single injection given into the muscle of the thigh or upper arm.

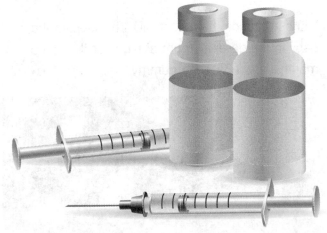

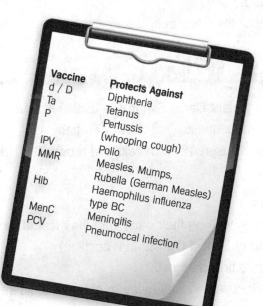

Vaccine	Protects Against
d / D	Diphtheria
Ta	Tetanus
P	Pertussis (whooping cough)
IPV	Polio
MMR	Measles, Mumps, Rubella (German Measles)
Hib	Haemophilus influenza type BC
MenC	Meningitis
PCV	Pneumoccal infection

Age	Vaccine
2 months	DTaP / IPV / Hib + pneumococcal conjugate vaccine (PCV)
3 months	DTaP / IPV / Hib + MenC vaccine
4 months	DTaP / IPV / Hib + MenC + pneumococcal conjugate vaccine (PCV)
12 months	Hib / MenC vaccine
13 months	MMR + pneumococcal conjugate vaccine (PCV)

Sleep and SIDS

Sleep Patterns

In the first months, babies are asleep more than they're awake.

Newborns (neonates) sleep for 16–20 hours a day, waking about every 4 hours to feed.

Seventy per cent of babies sleep through the night by 4 months, most by 6 months. At 12 months, being more active, they sleep at night without waking and have a daytime nap. By the age of 3 the daytime nap is discontinued, and night time sleep decreases.

Importance of Sleep

During sleep the body produces a growth hormone, and rests mentally and physically.

A routine calms children and makes them feel more secure.

In the run up to bedtime…
- reduce activity levels
- offer a warm bath and drink
- read a story
- recall the day's activities.

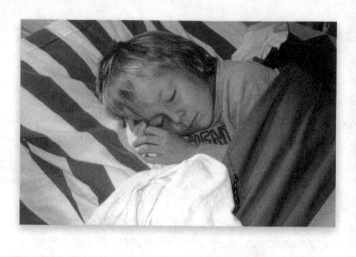

Sudden Infant Death Syndrome

Sudden Infant Death Syndrome (**SIDS**) is rare. It's the sudden, unexpected death of a baby as it sleeps. Measures can be taken to reduce the risk of SIDS.

Always…
- put a baby on their back with their feet at the end of the cot (feet-to-foot position)
- use a firm mattress
- tuck covers in well below a baby's shoulders
- ensure the room is 16–18°C
- seek medical advice if a baby is unwell
- breastfeed if possible.

Never…
- let anyone smoke in your home
- have a baby in bed with you (especially if you're tired, have drunk alcohol or taken drugs)
- put a cot near a radiator or in direct sunlight, or let a baby overheat
- cover a baby's head.

You can reduce the risk of SIDS by keeping the baby in the parents' room at night for the first 6 months, and offering a dummy.

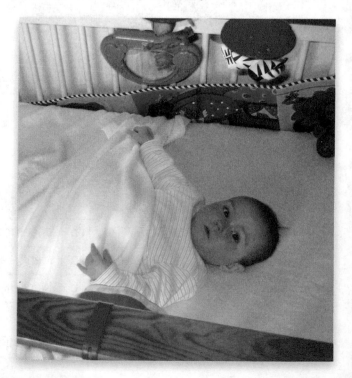

Fresh Air, Exercise and Sunlight

Fresh Air

To remain healthy, children need fresh air, exercise and sunlight.

Being in the **fresh air** outside…

- improves appetite
- promotes a good night's sleep
- encourages development of supple muscles when using tricycles, pedal cars, balls, hoops, etc.
- gives children more space to play and to let off steam.

Exercise

Exercise…

- improves general health
- strengthens muscles, especially heart and lung muscles
- gives children confidence in their abilities
- sets good patterns for future behaviour (active lifestyle, keeping fit)
- makes children feel good (improves self-esteem)
- strengthens bones
- reduces the risk of becoming overweight.

Sunlight

Ultraviolet (**UV**) **rays** from the sun on the skin produce Vitamin D. Over exposure to sunlight in childhood leads to an increased risk of adult cancer.

Use sunblock or high sun protection factor (SPF): 30+ on babies and 15+ on older children. Reapply regularly, especially after playing in water. Remember…

- **slip, slap, slop**
- **slip** on a shirt
- **slap** on a hat
- **slop** on the sunscreen.

Protect the back of the neck, feet and shoulders from the sun, especially when it's at its hottest. Keep babies in the shade or under a canopy / parasol. Special UV protective clothing can be bought, which blocks out UV rays.

KEY WORDS

Make sure you understand these words before moving on!

- Pre-admission visit
- Emergency admission
- Regression
- Protecting
- Vaccines
- Defence system
- Antibodies
- SIDS
- Fresh air
- Exercise
- UV rays

Clothing and Footwear

Clothes

Newborn baby clothes (layette) should be…
- lightweight, soft, non-irritant, and non-flammable
- appropriate for the weather / indoor temperature
- easy to put on and remove, e.g. envelope neck opening, and easy to access for nappy changing
- easy to wash / dry / iron.

Newborn clothes shouldn't have ribbons or open weave, which might trap fingers.

Older children's clothes should be…
- suitable for weather conditions / occasion
- hard wearing
- easy to wash / dry / iron
- fastened with Velcro or large buttons
- elasticated at the waist
- big enough to allow for growth and movement
- brightly coloured / chosen by the child.

Shoes

'Padders' (pre-walkers) protect babies' feet when they're crawling. They don't need shoes until they are walking. Feet should be measured regularly by trained fitters and when buying shoes, to make sure that shoes fit well.

Features of a good children's shoe are that they're lightweight, have no inside seams, have a low heel, flexible **slip-resistant** soles, adjustable fastening, and growing room.

Different footwear is worn depending on the occasion, e.g. pumps, slippers, wellies, trainers.

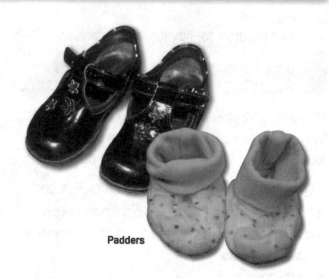

Padders

Nappies

Nappies can be disposable or reusable.

Advantages of **disposable nappies** are that…
- no washing is required; they're thrown away when used
- they're **absorbent**, reducing the possibility of nappy rash (ammonia dermatitis)
- they're easy to use
- they're available in different versions, e.g. boy / girl, day / night, pull-ups
- they come in different sizes, which ensures a good fit
- they're useful for travelling / on holiday.

The **disadvantage** of **disposable nappies** is that they're not environmentally friendly, because they aren't biodegradable. They may also be more expensive in the long run.

General Equipment

Baby equipment can be essential or desirable, depending on your lifestyle, budget, and the age of the child.

All equipment should be...
- safe, i.e. have a **Kitemark**
- strong and stable
- easy to assemble and use
- easy to clean
- checked regularly for damage

- suited to the size, age and any special needs of the child
- made from non-toxic material, which is durable and hardwearing.

Apart from transport, feeding and sleeping equipment, you may also need a changing mat, playpen, baby monitor, bouncing cradle, baby carrier, bath, steriliser, safety gate, car seat and reins.

All equipment should provide good value for money.

Transport

Factors to consider when **buying** a **pram, buggy** or **transport system** are...
- its brakes, suspension and tyres
- whether it's sturdy and stable
- its storage size / weight
- whether it's easy to adjust / fold

- whether to buy new or second hand
- comfort and safety
- versatility
- whether it's front / rear facing
- weather resistance
- manoeuvrability.

Feeding and Sleeping

High chairs should recline for babies who can't sit unaided. They should be stable, with a fitted safety harness, and easy to clean, with no sharp corners.

Booster seats can be used for older children.

Cots should have safety catches, adjustable mattress height, a snug fitting waterproof mattress, and bars 45–65mm apart.

Beds may need safety rails fitting.

Quick Test

1. What type of neck opening is best for newborn babies?
2. When do babies need shoes?
3. Traditional nappies are more environmentally friendly than disposable nappies. **True** or **false**?
4. What type of high chair is needed for a baby who can't sit unaided?

KEY WORDS

Make sure you understand these words before moving on!
- Slip-resistant
- Disposable nappies
- Absorbent
- Kitemark

Bathing and Washing

Bathing and Safety

Bathing and washing are an important part of a baby's routine. A baby can be bathed every day, or topped and tailed. Bath time should be an enjoyable, relaxing experience.

Make sure that your bathroom is **safe** by…
- always **supervising** and **never** leaving babies and children unattended
- having a wall-mounted, locked medicine cabinet
- keeping cosmetics, razors and cleaning materials out of reach
- teaching your baby/child to 'sit' in the bath
- having a slip-resistant bath/shower
- setting the hot water temperature no higher than 46°C
- putting cold water in the bath first
- covering the hot water tap with a face cloth or special cover.

Topping and Tailing

Every day, wash your baby's **face** (top) and **bottom** (tail). Have the equipment ready in a warm room (18–21°C) so your baby doesn't get cold. Remove your baby's clothes, except vest and nappy.

Start by gently wiping your baby's face with cotton wool and warm water. Use a fresh piece for each eye to avoid cross infection, wiping from the bridge of the nose outwards. Clean the creases in the neck where milk can gather.

Clean your baby's hands, remove the nappy and clean the genital area. Never pull a boy's foreskin. Clean a girl from front to back, so bacteria doesn't spread.

Bathing

You may bath your baby at any time. Start by topping and tailing. Then…
1. Fill the bath (cold water first, then add hot water).
2. Check the water temperature.
3. Wrap your baby in a warm towel, so body heat isn't lost. Wash their hair whilst supporting the baby's head and neck. This isn't necessary daily.
4. Dry hair.
5. Lower your baby into the bath, supporting their head and body.
6. Wash your baby.
7. Allow your baby to kick for enjoyment and exercise.
8. Lift your baby onto a towel. Pat the baby dry carefully to prevent sores developing in creases.
9. Dress your baby.

Remember that special products can be used as babies can have sensitive skin, but they aren't always needed.

Never poke your baby's nose or ears with cotton buds.

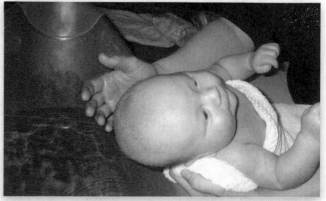

Children and Accidents

Accidents in the Home

Minor mishaps happen as children explore and experiment. Accidents are more likely to happen when children are excited, tired, upset or unsupervised. The amount of supervision you need to provide depends on the children's age, personality, and the activity.

Accident	Potential Hazard
Fall	Stairs, steps, window, pram, cot, bed, carpet
Choking	Sweets, nuts, small toy pieces, plastic bags, cords on curtains, blinds
Suffocation	Plastic bags, animals in bedroom, pillow (baby), discarded fridge / freezer
Cuts	Knives, scissors, tools, broken glass
Electrocution	Sockets, electrical equipment
Scalds and burns	Hot drinks, matches, lighters, fires, cookers, irons, radiators, bath
Poisoning	Cleaning / household chemicals, medicines, alcohols, garden chemicals, some plants, berries, fungi
Drowning	Bath, paddling pool, pond, buckets of water (2 / 3 cm is deep enough to cause death)

Age-related Accidents

Age	Mostly Likely Accident	Reason
Young baby	Bumps / falls	Wriggles, kicks, rolls over
6 months	Choking / suffocation	Holds objects, mouths (explores objects with mouth)
9–12 months (doesn't understand danger)	All types	Wants to touch, moves quickly
2 years (starts to understand danger)	Burns, poisoning, falls	Copies adults, wants to be independent
3 years (understands danger)	All types	Forgets because they're focused on activity
4 years	Falls, traffic	Plays outdoors, can't see cars or judge their speed and distance

Safety Symbols

The **safety symbols** you should look out for are the...

- **Kitemark**, which shows that the product meets the relevant standards and has been independently tested
- **CE mark**, which shows that the product has passed European Economic Community (EEC) standards
- **Lion Mark**, which means that toys have met British toy manufacturers' standards.

Lion Mark   Kitemark

Safety

Safety at Home

Follow these general **safety precautions** at home:
- Cover sockets.
- Use good lighting.
- Use fire guards and radiator guards.
- Use protective film or safety glass, and fit child-resistant window locks.
- Use door slam protectors.
- Don't have worn or damaged carpets.
- Use safety gates.
- Have tidy floors and stairs, and mop up spills.
- Install smoke and carbon dioxide alarms.

In the **kitchen**, keep sharp tools and glasses out of reach. Use the least toxic cleaning products, with child-resistant lids, and keep them locked away. Install safety catches on your washing machine, tumble dryer, fridge and freezer. Don't use table cloths, and **supervise very closely** if a child is 'helping'. Use a cooker guard, and keep pan handles facing inwards.

In the **living room**, have stable, solid furniture, and use corner guards. Put locks on the DVD / video player, and keep breakable ornaments and poisonous plants out of the reach of babies / children.

In the **bedroom**, keep your bed away from the window / radiator. Don't use hot water bottles or free standing heaters, and wear flame-resistant nightwear.

Safety Outside

When children are playing outside, make sure there are no broken walls or fences, and keep gates locked.

Remove animal faeces.

Garden tools and chemicals should be locked away. Make sure children wear safety helmets and protective clothing (like knee pads) when necessary, e.g. riding bikes. Use child-friendly garden products, and don't grow poisonous plants, e.g. laburnum. Remove, fence off or cover garden ponds / water features. Supervise barbecues and garden bonfires.

Clean the sandpit regularly and keep it covered. Check all garden toys regularly for wear and tear, and install them on a suitable surface, e.g. bark chippings for swings. Put trampolines on a flat surface with a net around them.

Play areas in **parks** should have…
- fenced-off equipment
- no rubbish or dog dirt
- swings with rubber seats or cradle seats for toddlers
- low-level climbing equipment
- slides set in banks or slopes
- regular maintenance checks.

Personal Safety

Without scaring children, parents should teach them about 'stranger danger' using suitable books, DVDs and role play. This message can be reinforced by nursery schools, playgroups, etc.

If children are lost, they should know to stand still and wait until they're found. They should say 'No' if anyone makes them feel uncomfortable, and tell a trusted adult immediately.

Car and Road Safety

Legally, **children travelling by car** must use the **correct safety restraint**, which should **conform to EEC regulations**. After a car accident, the seat should be replaced. Air bags should be immobilised if a child travels in the front seat.

You should…
- use child locks on car doors
- not leave your child unattended in a car
- fit child restraints correctly, and adjust them on every journey.

Choose a restraint for the **weight** and **size** of the child, rather than their age. Some restraints fit into more than one stage, because they can be converted.

Teach your child the dangers about traffic, and about the **Green Cross Code**, using books, games, and role play.

Practise **road safety** by…
- holding your child's hand across the road, or using reins / a wrist lead
- setting a good example
- making sure that your child wears bright, reflective clothing.

Stage	Group	Weight	Age	Other Information
1	0	Up to 10kg	Birth to 6 / 9 months	Use in the back and front of the car; often forms part
	0+	Up to 13kg	Birth to 12 / 15 months	of the transport system; accessories are available
2	1	9–18kg	9 months–4 years	Have an integral harness
3	2	15–25kg	4–6 years	Child is held in place with the adult seat belt

Supermarket Trolleys

Choose the correct supermarket trolley for your child's weight and age. Fasten your child into the seat securely, and don't leave unattended.

KEY WORDS
Make sure you understand these words before moving on!
- Supervising
- Safety symbols
- Safety precautions
- Green Cross Code

Practice Questions

1 Which of the following statements are correct? Tick the correct options.

A You should prick blisters on burns. ⬭

B Remove objects from the eye with an antiseptic wipe. ⬭

C Apply pressure to a deep wound. ⬭

D Use calamine lotion on scalds. ⬭

E Apply a cold compress to a bruise. ⬭

F To stop a nose bleed, hold the head backwards. ⬭

G Never remove an insect sting. ⬭

H Deep wounds never need stitches. ⬭

2 If your child is ill, when should you get help from the hospital? Tick the correct option.

A The child has no appetite. ⬭

B The child has breathing difficulties. ⬭

C The child has a temperature of 37°C. ⬭

D The child has been sick. ⬭

3 Explain how a vaccine is given.

_____

4 Choose the correct words from the options given to complete the following sentences.

non-emergency	equipment	pre-admission	play	reassure

A _____ visit for a _____ admission to hospital can

_____ children. They will be shown _____ and encouraged to

_____ with it.

5 What could be the effect of keeping a baby in the parents' bedroom at night for the first 6 months, and offering a dummy?

_____

6 Which of the following statements applies to clothing for a newborn baby? Tick the correct options.

   A Clothing should allow access for nappy changing. ☐

   B Clothing should be elasticated at the waist. ☐

   C Clothing should be brightly coloured. ☐

   D Clothing should be soft and non-irritant. ☐

   E Clothing should be easy to put on and remove. ☐

   F Clothing shouldn't have ribbons. ☐

   G Clothing should be pink for a girl and blue for a boy. ☐

   H Clothing should be easy to wash / dry / iron. ☐

7 Fill in the missing words to complete the following sentence.

Equipment can be _____ or _____ depending on lifestyle, budget,

and the age of the child.

8 The following statements are about bathing a baby. Circle the correct options in the following sentences.

   a) Fill the bath with **cold** / **hot** water first.

   b) **Pat** / **rub** the baby dry with a towel.

   c) **Always** / **never** use cotton buds to clean the ears.

   d) Using a fresh piece of cotton wool for each eye, clean the eye by wiping from the bridge of the nose **outwards** / **inwards**.

9 Which of the following doesn't potentially cause scalds and burns? Tick the correct option.

   A Hot drinks ☐

   B Bath ☐

   C Iron ☐

   D Plastic bag ☐

10 How can you teach the Green Cross Code and the dangers of traffic to children?

_____

_____

Early Years Foundation Stage

Early Years Foundation Stage

The Early Years Foundation Stage (EYFS) is a statutory (legal) framework introduced by the Department of Children, Schools and Families (DCSF). The framework sets standards for all children from **birth to 5 years** in **development**, **learning** and **care**.

These standards are monitored and checked by **Ofsted** (Office for Standards in Education), who do regular inspections and report back to parents and carers.

This framework must be used by all early years' providers who are registered with the local education authority (LEA), e.g. childminders, pre-schools.

A person can only be registered when they have clear health and police checks, and verified references. Premises are inspected for health and safety.

Providers must make provision for special educational needs, and be sympathetic to the needs of children from different ethnic, cultural and religious backgrounds.

Early Years Action (**EYA**) provides extra help for children who need it, e.g. extra adult help in the classroom. Targets may be written in an Individual Education Plan (**IEP**). EYA Plus provides extra professional help or resources where necessary, e.g. speech therapy.

EYFS Profile

The **EYFS profile** must be completed by all providers for each child in the academic year that they reach age 5. The profile is based on recorded observations of the 6 areas of learning from the **EYFS curriculum** 3–5. These are...
- personal, social and emotional development
- communication, language and literacy
- problem solving, reasoning and numeracy
- knowledge and understanding of the world
- physical development
- creative development.

The aim is that by the end of their first year in primary school, children will have achieved the Early Learning Goals.

Parents in Partnership

Parents can support the EYFS curriculum by providing activities at home.

Encourage **maths skills** by...
- **counting** – counting items around the home, singing counting rhymes
- **measuring** – filling and emptying containers, weighing baking ingredients
- **finding shapes** – everyday objects that are round, square, triangular, etc.

Encourage **reading** / **writing skills** by...
- **reading together** – pointing out letters and words
- **learning letters** – playing I-Spy games
- **making marks** on paper / chalkboards
- **bringing books to life** – using a 'story sack' containing 'props'.

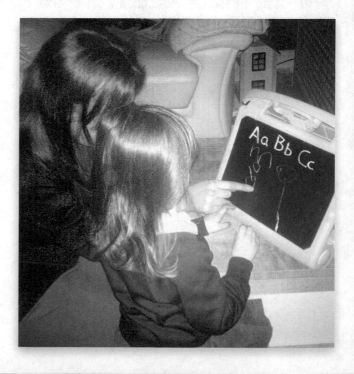

Child Care Options

Many mothers work, so choosing child care is important. Child care can be full-time or part-time. Some parents don't need any child care, but want their children to be looked after by other people to encourage socialisation, offer play opportunities, and to let parents have a break.

Child care can be **nursery group care** or **in-home care**. Benefits are available to help low income families with registered child care costs.

Every 3 and 4 year old is entitled to 15 hours of free early education a week. This can be delivered flexibly over a minimum of 3 days a week.

Parents can choose where they would like this learning to take place, e.g. nursery school, pre-school, private day nursery.

Babysitters

Babysitters are paid to look after children for a few hours, often in the evening, so parents can go out. Babysitters must know…

- where the parents are, what time they will be home, and how to contact them
- an emergency telephone number, e.g. for a grandparent or GP
- special words the child uses, e.g. for their comforter
- where the first aid box is
- the child's bedtime routine
- what food / drink the child is allowed
- about allergies the child has, or any medication they might need.

Crèches and Out of School Clubs

Children from **6 months** to **5 years** use **crèches**. The **advantages** of a **crèche** are…
- they're often attached to a workplace
- the cost of care may be subsidised by employers
- they're open all year round
- the child can go full- or part-time
- the parent can visit in their breaks
- socialisation with other children.

Crèches also have some **disadvantages**. They may be large and impersonal, child care can be a problem if a parent's job changes, and you can't send an ill child.

From **3 years upwards**, children can attend a **breakfast club** / **out of school club**.

The **advantages** of these clubs are that the child receives care before and after school, the clubs are attached to the school, and there are some qualified staff.

Some clubs extend their hours during school holidays.

The **disadvantages** are the cost, they aren't suitable for children under 3 years, and they have limited hours.

In-home Care

Relatives

Grandparents and / or other family members can provide care for children from birth onwards. Care by **relatives** has lots of **advantages**:

- one-to-one care
- familiar environment
- flexible hours
- close bond with the child
- can come to child's house
- child care is free
- it follows the child's routine

- understands child's personality
- can pick up / drop off at nursery
- experienced
- can look after the child, even when they're ill.

The **disadvantages** are that children can become too attached, they're physically demanding, and there's less opportunity to mix with other children. The family member's home may not be child proof, and it can put a strain on family relationships, because there may be conflicting views on child rearing.

Childminders

Childminders provide care for children from 3 months upwards. The **advantages** of a childminder are...

- flexible hours
- they're usually experienced
- they may have child care qualifications
- they can pick up / drop off at nursery
- homely environment
- the close bond with the child
- that they can adapt a routine to suit the child
- visits to places of interest
- siblings are kept together
- they can provide continuity of care, e.g. when the child starts school
- there are often other children to play with.

The **disadvantages** include the risk of infections from other children. Childminders can't look after ill children, and there's no back-up plan if your childminder is ill.

Nannies and Au pairs

Nannies look after children from birth onwards, usually in the child's home. The **advantages** of nannies are that they are usually qualified, and can work flexible hours. If they live in there are no travel costs, and they can look after all the children in the family.

The **disadvantages** of nannies are that they're very expensive, they may need their own room and there's a lack of privacy at home.

Au pairs are similar to nannies, but cheaper. The **advantages** of au pairs are that they can help children learn about another culture, they live in, and they work flexible hours. They also help with household tasks.

The **disadvantages** of au pairs are that they're not registered or monitored by Ofsted, and they may not be qualified or experienced. They also need their own room, and there's a lack of privacy at home. If they're from abroad, there may be language problems. They may only stay for a short time.

Nursery Group Care

Day Nurseries

Day nurseries provide care for children aged **3 months to 5 years**. Day nurseries have lots of **advantages**:

- all day care with long hours
- full-time or part-time care offered
- open all year round
- qualified staff
- children are grouped by age
- structured learning
- 100 percent reliable
- a range of toys

- indoor and outdoor play
- socialisation with other children
- good preparation for school.

It can be difficult to obtain a place at a day nursery. Other **disadvantages** are the cost, and the fact that day nurseries don't provide a homely environment. Children are given less individual attention, and there is often travel involved. Children are at a greater risk of infection, and you can't send an ill child. Siblings may not be together.

Pre-schools / Playgroups

Pre-schools and **playgroups** provide care for children aged from **2–5 years**. The **advantages** of this type of care are that there is some trained staff, the care is community based, and there is strong parental involvement. The children are all of a similar age, and they have an opportunity to socialise with each other.

The **disadvantages** of pre-schools and playgroups are the short session times, and that they're only open in term time.

Nursery Schools / Nursery Classes

Nursery schools / nursery classes provide care for children aged 3–5 years, and are part of the foundation stage.

The **advantages** of nursery schools / classes are that they're a good preparation for school, there is structured learning, and children are with their peers.

The **disadvantages** are that, like the pre-schools and playgroups, there are only short sessions available, and they only open in term time.

Quick Test

1. What do the letters Ofsted stand for?
2. The EYFS curriculum can be supported by parents. **True** or **false**?
3. Nursery schools provide full-time care. **True** or **false**?
4. There are no disadvantages if children are cared for by grandparents. **True** or **false**?

KEY WORDS

Make sure you understand these words before moving on!

- Ofsted
- IEP
- EYFS profile
- EYFS curriculum
- Crèche
- Breakfast club
- Nannies
- Au pairs
- Playgroups

Children with Special Needs

Children with Special Needs

Children with special needs have **permanently impaired health** (disability) or **learning difficulties**.

Children may have a congenital disorder, e.g. cystic fibrosis, or have suffered damage in the uterus from drugs, alcohol, smoking abuse or rubella. Children can also suffer damage during birth, e.g. brain damage, or damage after birth, e.g. an accident causing blindness, or meningitis, which can cause brain damage.

Disabilities may be...

- physical, e.g. blindness, deafness
- intellectual, e.g. autism, Down's syndrome, ADHD (attention deficit hyperactivity disorder)
- a combination of both
- severe or mild.

Disorder	Cause	Effect
Down's syndrome	Extra chromosome	Slanting eyes; eyelids with extra fold; single crease on palm; limited intelligence; large tongue; flatter head
Cystic fibrosis	Inherited gene	Daily physiotherapy is needed to prevent breathing difficulties and chest infections
Cerebral palsy	Brain damage	Difficulties with fine manipulative and gross motor skills
Muscular dystrophy	Inherited gene	A gradual weakening of muscles
Spina Bifida	Damage to spinal cord	Mobility problems
Autism	Brain damage	Social interaction and language difficulties; withdrawn, giving objects more attention than people; don't like changes; may be aggressive / gifted
Dyslexia	Possibly genetic	Reading / writing problems; letters appear to move, are confused or reversed

Toys

Children with disabilities may have **developmental delay**, i.e. they don't reach their milestones as expected. Toys can help with all areas of development. Normal toys are fine, but should match the stage of development rather than chronological (actual) age. Frequent changing of toys prevents boredom and provides stimulation.

Sensory impairment can be of the eyes (visual) or ears (aural). Toys can be used to compensate by encouraging the use of another sense, e.g. a visually impaired child could be encouraged to touch, feel and explore toys with textures and sounds. A child with a hearing impairment would benefit from toys that move or allow the child to feel vibrations, such as a musical instrument, e.g. a drum.

Gifted Children

Gifted children reach their intellectual milestones early and are academically able. They may have difficulty making friends and socialising.

Their physical, social and emotional development is usually the same as other children.

Children with Special Needs

Effects on the Family

Children with special needs have the same basic needs as all children. Depending on the severity of their disability, extra help may be needed in caring for them. This help can be provided by social services, voluntary organisations, or government.

Negative effects on the family are…
- that practical help is needed with mobility and hygiene
- the cost in providing an adapted home, equipment, toys, extra laundry facilities, car
- insensitivity from the wider community
- that social activities, e.g. holidays and days out, are difficult to organise
- finding suitable child care if returning to work, or a suitable babysitter
- that family members may become over protective or embarrassed
- that regular medical appointments take time.

There can also be a negative effect on siblings, because parents may have less time to play with them. They may feel jealous, or upset that their sibling is suffering. They can be teased by their peers, and have more responsibility in the home.

On the **positive side**, children with special needs can bring a family closer together (bonding), and they can help siblings to be more tolerant of others.

Voluntary Organisations

Many organisations help special needs children and their families. They include…
- **NDCS** – National Deaf Children's Society
- **RNIB** – Royal National Institute of Blind People
- **RNID** – Royal National Institute for the Deaf
- **Scope** – for people with cerebral palsy
- **NAS** – The National Autistic Society
- **ASBAH** – Association for Spina Bifida and Hydrocephalus
- **CF Trust** – Cystic Fibrosis Trust
- **British Dyslexia Association**.

Quick Test

1. Disabilities can be severe or mild. **True** or **false**?
2. What do the letters ADHD stand for?
3. What kind of sensory impairment is a problem with eyesight?
4. Should toys for children with disabilities match their stage of development or chronological age?

KEY WORDS

Make sure you understand these words before moving on!
- Down's syndrome
- Autism
- Dyslexia
- Developmental delay

Helping Families

Helping Families

Local authorities, health authorities, social services, national and local voluntary organisations work together to provide services for families.

Examples of **national voluntary organisations** are...
- Barnardo's
- Gingerbread
- Home-Start.

Local voluntary organisations include...
- church groups
- community groups.

Support and friendship for families

Believe in children
Barnardo's
Registered Charity Nos: 216250 and SC037605

Gingerbread
Single parents, equal families

Sure Start

Sure Start is a government programme that provides a wide range of **integrated** services in the local community.

A range of professionals share their expertise to work with parents and children to meet their needs.

Its services include...
- family support
- support with employment
- health services
- care
- education.

All of this support is available from a single point of contact.

Financial Benefits

Some **benefits** are available to everyone, regardless of income. Others are 'means' tested (i.e. they depend on individual family circumstances).

Benefits include...
- Sure Start Maternity Grant
- Statutory Maternity Pay
- child benefit
- baby bonds (Child Trust Fund)
- reduced price formula milk
- free milk and vitamins and school meals
- New Deal for Lone Parents schemes
- Child Support Maintenance (CSA)
- free dental treatment, prescriptions and eye tests for pregnant women
- Disability Living Allowance

- Carers' Allowance
- Welfare to Work
- Care to Learn
- Sixth Form College
- Working Families' Tax Credit
- income support
- housing and Council Tax benefit.

HM Revenue & Customs
Website:
www.hmrc.gov.uk/childbenefit

national savings & investments
ns&i

National Savings and Investments Blackpool

Child Benefit

If you get in touch with us, tell us reference

F&C Child Trust Fund Centre
Block C, Western House
Lynchwood Business Park
Peterborough PE2 6BP
Telephone 0845 600 3030
Facsimile +44 0300 7410 9008
E-mail investor.enquiries@fandc.com

Child Trust Fund

Health Visitors

Health visitors work with every family who has a **child under 5**.

They visit mothers in the post-natal period and give them emotional support. They also organise and run baby clinics and post-natal groups. They advise on health matters, feeding problems and behavioural difficulties. They also monitor growth, and do developmental assessments. These are recorded in the 'red book', which all mothers are given.

Health visitors also advise on family problems, e.g. domestic violence.

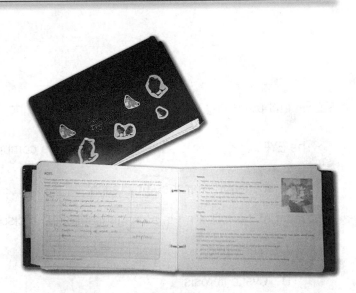

Social Services

Social services **register** and **check EYFS providers**, e.g. childminders and nurseries. They work with families who have problems, and involve other agencies as necessary to prevent children going into care.

Where **child protection** or **violence** is an issue, they monitor and assess the situation to make sure that children aren't at risk. They remove children from the environment if necessary.

Social services take children into care, either temporarily or permanently, if parents aren't able to look after them. They also arrange long- and short-term foster care. They are involved in the adoption process and support adopted children and their families.

Social services also help with **parenting problems**. They give advice and support and run parenting classes.

They help parents and carers with **financial problems**. They tell people what benefits are available. They encourage people who are apathetic, embarrassed, or want to keep their independence, to claim benefits to which they are entitled.

Social services staff also help with **filling in forms**, e.g. benefit forms, if they're complicated to understand, or if there's a language difficulty.

Quick Test

1. Where are Sure Start services found?
2. Health visitors work with families who have a child under 5. **True** or **false**?
3. Who arranges foster care?
4. Do people always know what benefits are available to them?

KEY WORDS
Make sure you understand these words before moving on!
- Sure Start
- Benefits
- Health visitors

Practice Questions

1 Who must use the framework of the Early Years Foundation Stage?

_____

_____

2 Fill in the missing words to complete the following sentence.

The EYFS _____ must be completed by all _____ for each child

in the academic year that they reach _____.

3 Which of the following is a congenital inherited disorder? Tick the correct option.

A Meningitis ⬭

B Cystic fibrosis ⬭

C Rubella ⬭

D Accidental brain damage ⬭

4 Choose the correct words from the options given to complete the following sentence.

| **government** | **range** | **local** | **Sure Start** | **integrated** |

_____ is a _____ programme, which

provides a _____ of _____ services in the _____

community.

5 Which of the following are in-home types of child care? Tick the correct options.

A Crèche ⬭

B Grandparent ⬭

C Day nursery ⬭

D Pre-school ⬭

E Nanny ⬭

F Breakfast club ⬭

G Playgroup ⬭

H Au pair ⬭

6 Choose the correct words from the options given to complete the following sentences.

3 months–5 years   **2–5**   **3–5**   **3 years upwards**

Day nursery is suitable for ages _____. Breakfast club is suitable for children

aged _____. Pre-school / playgroup is suitable for _____ years.

Nursery school is suitable for _____ years.

7 Circle the correct options in the following sentences.

a) Children with Down's syndrome have **daily physiotherapy** / **limited intelligence**.

b) Children with Spina Bifida have **mobility problems** / **slanting eyes**.

c) Children with autism find **walking** / **social interaction** difficult.

d) Children with dyslexia have **reading problems** / **chest infections**.

8 Which of the following statements are true? Tick the correct options.

A Au pairs are similar to nannies.

B Breakfast clubs can be attached to schools.

C Nannies can't work flexible hours.

D You can send an ill child to nursery.

E Relatives can care for a child in their own home.

F Au pairs live in.

G Crèches are often attached to work places.

H Nursery schools have to be paid for.

Answers

Family and Parenthood

Quick Test Answers

Page 5
1. Parents and children live together in a nuclear family.
2. Primary and secondary socialisation.
3. Carers
4. True

Page 7
1. Nature and nurture.
2. True
3. Yes
4. Because they want to be grandparents.

Page 8
1. Contraception is the deliberate prevention of a pregnancy.
2. False
3. NFP (natural family planning).
4. Coitus interruptus.

Answers to Practice Questions

Page 10–11
1. A family is the basic unit of society.
2. D
3. A, B, F, H.
4. nature, nurture.

5. Emergency contraception is needed after unprotected sex.
6. Natural family planning, infertile, menstrual cycle, not.
7.

Method of Contraception	What it Looks Like
Femidom	
Mini pill	
Male condom	
Contraceptive injection	
IUD	
Contraceptive implant	
Diaphragm	

8. B, C, E, H.

Pregnancy and Ante-natal Care

Quick Test Answers

Page 15
1. Semen is a mixture of sperm and seminal fluid.
2. Eggs are stored in the ovaries.
3. True
4. A fertilised egg implants itself in the uterus.
5. A sperm.

Page 17
1. False.
2. Babies become viable after 24 weeks.
3. EDD stands for estimated delivery date.
4. 37–42 weeks.
5. Identical twin.

Page 19
1. A bra worn in pregnancy should have wide straps.
2. Alcohol causes FAS (foetal alcohol syndrome).
3. False.
4. Gynaecologist
5. IVF stands for *in vitro* fertilisation.
6. ICSI stands for intra-cytoplasmic sperm injection.

Page 21
1. The baby is fully formed at Week 12.
2. False
3. The placenta, umbilical cord and amniotic sac are made by the fertilised egg.
4. True.
5. The amniotic sac is filled with amniotic fluid.

Page 23
1. High blood pressure in pregnancy could indicate pre-eclampsia.
2. False
3. Down's syndrome.

Page 25
1. The midwife does the booking-in visit.
2. False
3. The mother keeps the hand held notes in pregnancy.
4. No
5. Obstetrician

Answers to Practice Questions

Page 26–27
1. B
2. a) ovaries b) testes c) cervix d) penis e) vagina f) uterus g) sperm h) epididymis.
3. Pre-conceptual care should begin before conception.
4. single, two, identical.
5. A, E, F.
6.

Test	What it Does
Triple test	Measures AFP
Amniocentesis	Detects the baby's sex
Nuchal fold translucency	Measures fluid on the back of the neck
Blood test	Checks for anaemia

7. A hand held scanner over the abdomen, which is covered in gel, reflects sound waves, which project an image onto a screen.
8. C
9. **In any order:** be present at the birth, offer reassurance, let the midwife know his partner's wishes.

Answers

Birth and Postnatal Care

Quick Test Answers

Page 29
1. The midwife delivers a sealed sterile birth pack.
2. At the time of a home birth the midwife brings the necessary drugs and oxygen.
3. True
4. True

Page 31
1. An epidural must be given by an anaesthetist.
2. Pethidine.
3. False
4. No
5. 37°C

Page 35
1. The uterus, cervix and vagina form the birth canal.
2. True
3. Induction
4. False
5. After a Caesarean section recovery takes up to six weeks.

Page 37
1. Premature babies are looked after in a SCBU or NICU.
2. False
3. An incubator.
4. False

Page 39
1. The umbilical cord drops off 7–10 days after birth.
2. The average weight of a newborn baby is approximately 3.5kg.
3. The Moro reflex is also called the falling reflex.
4. Most babies score 7 or above on the Apgar test.
5. False

Answers to Practice Questions

Page 40–41
1. The Domino Delivery Scheme is when the midwife accompanies the mother to hospital, delivers the baby, and returns home with them six hours later.
2. **a)** entonox **b)** TENS **c)** epidural anaesthetic **d)** water birth **e)** pethidine **f)** epidural anaesthetic **g)** entonox **h)** pethidine.
3. Labour is the process of giving birth.
4. irregular, uterus, 1 minute, relaxes.
5.

Birth Position	Description
a) Transverse	Baby lies across the uterus
b) Oblique	Baby lies at an angle in the uterus
c) Breech	Baby has legs or bottom first

6. A, C, D, E, F, H.
7. Bonding is the feelings of love and affection between parent and child.
8. B

Nutrition and Health

Quick Test Answers

Page 43
1. Protein is needed for growth and repair.
2. The Food Standards Agency (FSA) has provided the eatwell plate guidelines.
3. True
4. An allergy is more serious.

Page 45
1. True
2. Yes
3. Formula (modified cows' milk), or a soya-based formula.
4. Cooled boiled water.

Page 47
1. Weaning is another word for mixed feeding.
2. True
3. 9–12 months
4. No

Page 49
1. False
2. Remove it without comment.
3. Yes
4. Nails should be kept short and clean.

Answers to Practice Questions

Page 50–51
1. B
2. **a)** Vitamin A **b)** Vitamin C **c)** iron **d)** fluoride.
3. **a)** calories, confectionery, children, target market.
   b) Government, legislation, advertising.
4. colostrum, clear, yellow.
5. G
6. chew, teeth, lumps.
7. D
8. **a)** too much **b)** aren't hungry **c)** teething **d)** don't.
9. Food poisoning can be prevented by the correct preparation, cooking and storage of food.

Areas of Development

Quick Test Answers

Page 53
1. True
2. Intellectual development is linked with learning.
3. Hypothesis
4. Time and volume are examples of concepts.

Page 55
1. 15 months.
2. Babies communicate by crying.
3. Echolalia is used at 6 months.
4. Telegraphic speech is used at 2 years.

Answers

Areas of Development (cont.)

Page 57
1. Large muscles.
2. Another name for fine motor skills is fine manipulative skills.
3. 6 months.
4. 2 years.
5. False

Page 59
1. Positive and negative ways.
2. 15 months.
3. 2 years.
4. False

Page 61
1. True
2. 6 months.
3. 3 years.
4. False

Page 63
1. False
2. Solitary play.
3. Cooperative play.
4. Physical play.

Answers to Practice Questions
Page 64–65
1. B
2. Intellectual
3. **a)** gurgles **b)** adah **c)** telegraphic speech **d)** 2000+.
4. 2 year, 12 month, 15 month, 9 month.
5. B
6. **In any order:** imaginative, pretend, role, superhero.
7. B, D, E, G.
8. skipping rope, sit-and-ride horse, mobile, stacking.
9. **a)** social **b)** physical **c)** exploratory **d)** manipulative **e)** role **f)** creative.

Health and Safety

Quick Test Answers
Page 67
1. True
2. Headlice are spread through head-to-head contact.
3. False
4. Threadworms are visible in faeces.

Page 69
1. Mumps
2. Pertussis
3. False
4. The risk of convulsions (fits).

Page 73
1. No
2. SIDS stands for Sudden Infant Death Syndrome.
3. Outside
4. True

Page 75
1. Envelope neck opening.
2. When they can walk.
3. True
4. A reclining high chair.

Page 79
1. True
2. Scalding
3. You would find a Lion Mark on toys.
4. EEC regulations.
5. True

Answers to Practice Questions
Page 80–81
1. C, E.
2. B
3. By giving an injection.
4. pre-admission, non-emergency, reassure, equipment, play.
5. The risk of SIDS is reduced.
6. A, D, E, F, H.
7. **In any order:** essential, desirable.
8. **a)** cold **b)** pat **c)** never **d)** outwards.
9. D
10. You can teach the dangers by using books, games, role play or by practising doing it.

Community Support

Quick Test Answers
Page 85
1. Office for Standards in Education.
2. True
3. False
4. False

Page 87
1. True
2. ADHD stands for attention deficit hyperactivity disorder.
3. Visual impairment.
4. Stage of development.

Page 89
1. Sure Start services are found in the local community.
2. True

3. Social services arrange foster care.
4. No

Answers to Practice Questions
Page 90–91
1. All early years' registered providers must use the framework, e.g. childminders, pre-schools, nurseries.
2. profile, providers, 5.
3. B
4. Sure Start, government, range, integrated, local.
5. B, E, H.
6. 3 months–5 years, 3 years upwards, 2–5, 3–5.
7. **a)** limited intelligence **b)** mobility problems **c)** social interaction **d)** reading problems.
8. A, B, E, F, G.

Index

Index

ACKNOWLEDGEMENTS

The authors and publisher are grateful to the copyright holders for permission to use quoted materials and images.

p.6 ©iStockphoto.com / Jani Bryson. **p.8** ©iStockphoto.com.
p.17 ©iStockphoto.com / Natalia Vasina Vladimirovna.
p.18 ©iStockphoto.com / Kirill Zdorov. **p.19** ©iStockphoto.com / Tatiana Gladskikh. **p.22** ©iStockphoto.com / Bojan Fatur. **p.28** ©istockphoto.com / Amanda Rohde. 'Preparing for a home birth' photograph reproduced with kind permission from Cynthia Luxford, LDM, CPM, www.homesweethomebirth.com.
p.29 ©istockphoto.com / Sawomir Jastrzbski. **p.30** ©iStockphoto.com.
p.32 ©iStockphoto.com / Monika Adamczyk. ©iStockphoto.com / Russell Tate. **p.35** ©iStockphoto.com. **p.36** ©iStockphoto.com. ©istockphoto.com / Dr. Heinz. Linke. **p.37** ©iStockphoto.com / Don Bayley. **p.38** ©iStockphoto.com. **p.42** eatwell plate (Food Standards Agency) © Crown copyright material is reproduced with the permission of the Controller of HMSO and Queen's Printer for Scotland. **p.46** ©iStockphoto.com / Rich Hobson. ©iStockphoto.com / Anthony Rosenberg. **p.48** ©2008 Jupiterimages Corporation. **p.49** ©iStockphoto.com. **p.52** ©iStockphoto.com / David Hernandez. **p.60** ©istockphoto.com / Sean Locke.
p.61 ©iStockphoto.com / Anthony Rosenberg. **p.62** Kitchen accessory set packaging reproduced with kind permission from Early Learning Centre, www.elc.co.uk. **p.70** ©iStockphoto.com / Julien Grondin.

p.71 ©istockphoto.com **p.74** ©iStockphoto.com / Eric Isselée, Brian McEntire. **p.77** Lion Mark reproduced with kind permission from The British Toy & Hobby Association, www.btha.co.uk. Kitemark reproduced with kind permission from BSI Product Services, www.kitemark.com.
p.87 Association for Spina Bifida and Hydrocephalus logo reproduced with kind permission from the Association for Spina Bifida and Hydrocephalus, www.asbah.org, helpline number: 0845 450 7755. RNIB logo reproduced with kind permission from Royal National Institute of Blind People, www.rnib.org.uk. CF Trust logo reproduced with kind permission from the Cystic Fibrosis Trust, www.cftrust.org.uk. NAS logo reproduced with kind permission from The National Autistic Society, www.autism.org.uk. NDCS logo reproduced with kind permission from the National Deaf Children's Society, www.ndcs.org.uk, NDCS Freephone Helpline: 0808 800 8880 (voice and text). **p.88** Barnardo's logo reproduced with kind permission from Barnardo's, www.barnardos.org.uk. Home-Start logo reproduced with kind permission from Home-Start, www.home-start.org.uk. Gingerbread logo reproduced with kind permission from Gingerbread, www.gingerbread.org.uk

With thanks to Andrea Brewis and Amanda Firth for proofreading the revision guide. The publishing team would also like to say a special thank you to the children who feature in the revision guide: Jessica, James, Lucy, Edward, Ellie, William, Georgia, Thomas, Imogen, Ella and Isaac.